The Decline of Working-Class Politics

The Decline
of
Working-Class Politics

Barry Hindess

MacGibbon & Kee

Granada Publishing Limited

First published 1971 by MacGibbon & Kee Ltd

3 Upper James Street, Golden Square, London W1R 4BP

Copyright © Barry Hindess 1971

ISBN 0 261 63210 8

Made and printed in Great Britain by
Hazell Watson & Viney Ltd., Aylesbury, Bucks
Set in Monotype Ehrhardt

This book is for its subjects: for those who have learnt that politics as we know it is not for them and for the many who have yet to learn this hard lesson; for the active and the passive whom I interviewed or merely talked with; for all those who helped in the preparation or the writing; for the masses who are simply other people.

Contents

Introduction

There is one obvious sense in which working-class politics has declined in the last twenty years or so: the proportion of working-class people involved at various levels of party politics has dropped. This change is perhaps most clearly visible at the parliamentary level where, after the 1951 election thirty-seven per cent of the Parliamentary Labour Party came from working-class backgrounds. By 1966 this figure had dropped to thirty per cent. Ministers from working-class backgrounds provided about half the membership of the Attlee cabinets in the 1940s. In 1964 the proportion was twenty-six per cent and it has since fallen to seventeen per cent in 1966, to nine per cent by the end of 1967[1] and to zero following the ministerial reshuffle of October 1969.

Similar, though on the whole less visible, changes have occurred at the local government level and also, as I shall argue later, among the grass-roots party activists. This latter is most noticeable at large party gatherings. Many commentators have noted, for example, that the physical appearance of the Labour Party in conference has changed over the years. Writing of the 1969 party conference in Brighton, the *Times* correspondent points out that:

The danger to the Tories is symbolised by the very appearance of the Labour conference which now looks very much more like a Conservative gathering than it did ten years ago. The class gap is closing: cloth caps are gone: even the pipe smoke seems to belch out less acridly at a Labour conference than it once did. This year's Labour chairman, Mrs Eirene White, could, by her manner of keeping the conference in its place, have done very well as a Tory lady chairman.[2]

On the other hand the title refers to a change in the nature of the Labour/Conservative polarization of formal politics: in particular to the fact that it is increasingly difficult to interpret this polarization in class terms. Here the decline is that of the proportion who are active in party politics because of their identification with, and commitment to the interests of, the working class as such.

I do not wish to suggest here that class is no longer significant, that we are all middle class (or working class) now. What has changed rather is the nature of the party political game. Elements of a class polarization of politics can still be seen at the level of electoral support and, to a far lesser extent, at the level of active membership. At the level of policy or of policy pronouncement, however, class polarization has declined markedly since the war and remains now only in touches of rhetoric to be produced on suitably solemn occasions. This does not mean that there are no longer any differences between the parties but rather that such differences as exist cannot be ranged along a class dimension. Furthermore, as I shall argue later, these differences do not relate to the interests of substantial sections of the population.

Class differences persist but do not find expression in the differences between the two major parties. To a large extent, of course, this has always been the case, but the Labour Party now appears to be less of a (working) class party than at any time in its history. This appearance is important for if Labour does not appear to be a class party the inter-party dispute cannot be presented in class terms. It is therefore becoming increasingly difficult to support one or other major party on the basis of class loyalty – to support Labour because one is working class, or the Conservatives because one is not. People may of course find other reasons for being active in party politics.

It is a major theme of this book that these two types of change, in the personnel of politics and in the nature of the Labour/Conservative dichotomy, are intimately related; that they are aspects of wider developments in the overall character of contemporary politics. Some of these developments and their wider implications, particularly at the grass-roots level of politics, will be examined in the following chapters.

The first two chapters provide a background for the later, more substantive sections. Chapter One deals, at a very general level, with the question of how one accounts for changes in political behaviour. Here it will be argued that any explanation must be in terms both of the meanings this behaviour has for the people concerned and of the social and political structure within which they act – their position within, say, the Labour Party, the relationships between their local party and other parties, and so on. In particular it is not sufficient to consider simply the overt action, for similar overt action (voting Labour) can mean a very different thing for the voters of, say, Ebbw Vale and South Kensington. The ways in which apparently non-political features of an individual's situation can affect his political action will also be discussed.

Chapter Two deals with a model of the development of Social Democratic Parties. This model, derived from the work of Roberto Michels, provides a framework for the analysis of the interrelationships of the party, its members and its potential supporters. In particular Michels' model has important implications for the reciprocal interdependence of party power structure, party policy, and the pattern of party membership.

These implications are documented and examined in greater detail in the following three chapters, with particular reference to the position of the city party. Chapter Three opens with a brief examination of the development and present characteristics of different types of area within the city and considers the position of the Labour Party in these areas. At first sight the relationship between activity in the party and the urban environment seems fairly straight-forward: the party organization is, on the whole, strongest in the more middle-class areas of the city and weakest in the most working-class areas.

However, as later chapters make clear, ward parties in the middle-class areas were smaller, and often non-existent, in the early 1950s while in the more working-class areas ward parties were generally larger, or at least more active, and some which existed then have since vanished. Thus any attempt to use the present situation as evidence of some timeless relationship between politics and urban structure is doomed to be misleading.

The following chapter examines some of the differences of interest, of political concerns, and of overall orientations towards politics between the different areas. Of particular significance here are the political meanings of the housing situation in the various areas, and differences in the way the party is experienced by members in Labour and non-Labour areas. In all cases the differences of political interest or concern and of general orientation towards politics will be related to the experiences of the people concerned.

This discussion provides the basis for an examination of the processes of change at the grass-roots level of Labour politics. Here I shall argue that there has been a vicious circle of decline in political activity in the more working-class areas of cities with a consequent shift of power within the local party towards the more middle-class areas. This in turn affects party policy and leads to a further decline in the more working-class areas. This process, whereby political power at the city level becomes concentrated in the middle-class areas, results in the appearance of a substantial degree of consensus between the different parties and in the political isolation of substantial sections of the population.

Although the discussion here remains largely at the level of grass-roots politics it is necessary also to consider the position of the national or regional party organization – both because higher levels of the party often intervene in local disputes and because widespread changes at the grass-roots level can affect these higher levels and, through these, the political environment of other local parties.

Chapter Six provides, in effect, an extended footnote to the preceding lengthy discussion of the city party. It contains, on the one hand, an all too brief examination of the role of sects and factions in the above developments and, on the other, some comments on the situation outside the cities, with particular emphasis on the importance of Nationalist Parties in Wales or Scotland as alternative foci of political allegiance.

The remainder of the book attempts to set these developments at the grass-roots level of politics in the context of the political implications of the increasing centralization of the British economy. The relations between political and economic developments are considered at two levels. At one level it is argued that the changes in the power structure of the Labour Party, and of British politics in general, can only be understood in terms of the changing economic structure. In particular the continuing growth of large commercial or industrial organizations, of large international firms, and of government management of the economy, has led to, and has depended upon, the development of close relationships between particular state organizations on the one hand and particular commercial or industrial organizations on the other. This of course affects the major political parties both in terms of the decisions they take and in terms of the way in which they take these decisions.

At another level, political and economic developments are related simply because they both affect the everyday environment of people at the grass-roots level. Political decisions may, for example, affect both the absolute number of houses available and the whole nature of the housing market and thereby affect the real housing choices open to many individuals. Or, to take another example, the actions of various planning bodies can affect the lives of large numbers of people in a more or less direct fashion. Continuing economic changes affect both the working conditions and the job security of increasing numbers of individuals.

Those affected by these changes or who fear that they may be affected develop new political concerns and perhaps new orientations towards politics. In particular, developments at all levels of the political and economic system involve the growth of different types of political apathy and of different types of estrangement from politics: ranging from a rejection of politics as such to a more straightforward distrust of politicians.

Finally the concluding chapter contains an attempt to assess the future shape of British politics. With the increasing centralization of political and economic decision making and the growing estrangement from party politics it seems likely that the forms of parliamentary democracy will increasingly appear to be both empty and irrelevant in years to come. To a large extent every electoral system is a sort of confidence trick and the maintenance of legitimacy through such tricks is a basic concern of all governments. When these tricks fail, as they are increasingly likely to, governments can be expected to resort to other measures.

Before proceeding with the examination of working-class, and specifically Labour, politics in Britain it is necessary to comment briefly on two issues: the systematic ambiguity of the words 'politics' and 'political'; the type of analysis to be attempted in the following pages.

On the first issue it is clear, I think, that in normal, everyday usage politics is to do with the activities of governments or political parties or, somewhat more generally, with the sorts of issue that political parties concern themselves with. Politics in this sense is more or less synonymous with party politics. As against this there is a broader conception in which politics pertains to the social structuring of power and its uses.

The difference here is not simply a matter of definition, of some people agreeing to use the word in one way and others using it differently. There is a strong normative element in the identification of politics with party politics. That is: 'political' issues are ones which are the proper subject for public debate, and political organizations (parties, local or national governments) provide the proper machinery for trying to do something about these issues.

It is because of this normative element that the dividing line between the political and the non-political is so significant. If two groups of people draw the line in different places and act accordingly, then one group will do things which the other would rule out as illegitimate – as not the right way to go about things, or as concerned with something which is no business of theirs anyway. Often those who step outside the normal bounds of politics are seen as 'politically motivated men' in the derogatory sense of this expression.

The broader one's conception of politics, the more aspects of society become (potentially) open to question. This questioning need by no means remain purely academic. If, for example, management–worker relationships are conceived of as political, then they are open to dispute and can be changed. To see an issue as political, in other words, is to admit that in this respect the present situation cannot be taken for granted. Some, of course, wish to maintain things as they are, some (politically motivated men) wish to change them. Others, for whom these things are non-political, simply take the present situation for granted: the question of change does not even arise.

Of course these few remarks barely scratch the surface of the problem here. Nevertheless it should be clear that, in the broader sense of the term, the drawing of the line between the political and the non-political is itself a political act. Furthermore, even the politically apathetic are, in a sense, politically active for in this latter sense there is no abdication from politics. At most one can abdicate from the recognition of the political nature of one's action.

My title uses the narrower, everyday, sense of politics.

15

This book, however, is concerned with both types of politics and with the relationships between the two* – with, in other words, the political significance of the decline of working-class politics. Sometimes politics will be used in one sense, sometimes in another. The context should make it clear which is intended.

Only two more points need be added in this introductory section. The first is that I have not attempted any sort of blow-by-blow account of political change. The following chapters are concerned rather with identifying some of the processes involved in this change and with their wider significance. In particular many developments in post-war British politics will be ignored or given a very cursory treatment. The fact that particular developments are not mentioned here does not mean that I consider them unimportant. On the contrary, the emphasis is on aspects of British politics which have, on the whole, been ignored by most contemporary sociologists and political scientists – or at least by those who are the recognized authorities on politics in Britain. For this reason the present account is necessarily a little one-sided; it does not pretend to give the whole picture.

My concern in this book is with the grass-roots of politics, with the masses, the man in the street – particularly with the working-class man in the street. It is remarkable how little attention has been given to grass-roots politics in view of the rapid growth of political science and political sociology in the last few years. From time to time, of course, researchers have descended upon the rank-and-file of politics to ask them how they voted or would vote, what they think about this or that issue, how their fathers or mothers voted, what sort of job they have, where they live, and so on. This doesn't take long and the rank-and-file are soon left to go about their business in peace until a new election draws near

---

* This aspect will assume increasing significance from Chapter Four onwards.

or, if they live too near to a university, a new research project gets underway.

Such snapshot views of the grass-roots tells us little, although they may tell us something, about how politics is lived or experienced by ordinary people, about what politics means to them. Generally speaking, the real stuff of politics is thought to exist at a more elevated level – local councillors or local party officials upwards. The masses, the rank-and-file, provide the background, the field on which the game of politics is played. In this sense the study of politics is in much the same state as, according to Lynd, is the study of American History. 'I think we know as much about the role of the common man in American History as we would know about Watts if the McCone Commission were our only source. . . . History has been written by elitists who assumed that when the common man acted as he did so for irrational reasons, or because he was manipulated in some way.'[3]

Those who hold such assumptions are concerned with the rank-and-file only in the sense that a referee or groundsman may be concerned with the state of the pitch. Otherwise they are naturally more interested in the higher levels of politics, in those who do the manipulating. This emphasis, I would argue, leads them to ignore many significant developments until, like the (perhaps temporary) collapse of Labour support after the 1966 elections, they burst upon the unsuspecting pundit out of a clear blue sky.

This is not the place to give such arguments and corresponding counter arguments the attention they deserve but these remarks do lead on to my second, and final, introductory point. Quite simply there is remarkably little evidence concerning grass-roots politics (below the level of the council chamber) or of changes therein. Records are often unavailable or unreliable and accounts of the past given by, say, full-time party officials often contradict those given by one-time party activists.*

Much of the following discussion is, therefore, unavoid-

* These problems of evidence are discussed at length in Chapter Five.

ably tentative. The few tables used in the text reflect the situation in Liverpool in 1964–5 and are intended primarily to illustrate the argument. As far as other cities are concerned my claim is not that the same situation exists but that similar processes have occurred: it is these processes that matter; the precise details are less important.

There is a story, certainly apocryphal, concerning a confrontation between C. Wright Mills and Paul Lazarsfeld. Mills reads the opening sentence of his book *The Sociological Imagination*: 'Nowadays men often feel that their private lives are a series of traps'. Lazarsfeld immediately replies: 'How many men, which men, how long have they felt this way, which aspects of their private lives bother them, do their public lives bother them, when do they feel free rather than trapped, what kinds of traps do they experience, etc., etc.?'[4]

No professional sociologist can write a sentence, let alone a paragraph, without going through some condensed version of such a dialogue. The reader will soon discover that many of Lazarsfeld's questions remain unanswered. There is no reason in principle to suppose that they cannot be answered – although in this case it is painstaking historical research rather than survey analysis that is called for. The practical problems, however, are likely to prove considerable. Already, I suspect, much of the recent past is lost to us: often the only traces remaining are in the records of the manipulators. To wait till all the facts were in would not be caution: it would be the height of irresponsibility.

1 Working-Class Political Behaviour

Studies of voting in Britain have, until very recently, given overwhelming support to the view that Britain is a society in which class is especially important as a determinant of political behaviour.[1] Study after study had shown that, minor variations apart, two-thirds of working-class voters supported Labour. Labour, it seemed, was the natural political home of the working class and only the deviant, Conservative, minority constituted a particular problem for sociologists or political scientists. Thus, while there have been several attempts to account for 'the working-class Tory'* it has not seemed necessary to account for working-class Labour voting. On the contrary this latter has been taken for granted and only deviations from the apparent norm were seen as problematic.

The importance of this assumption that the working class naturally vote Labour can be seen in the explanations proposed for voting behaviour. McKenzie and Silver locate their explanation of working-class conservatism explicitly in deviant psychological orientations towards politics. The deviants are either deferential or secular in their orientation. The former, as the name implies, are those who are primarily deferential towards the upper classes and who see the Conservative Party as the party of those who are born, or trained, to rule – anyone else is bound to make a mess of it. Secular voters, on the other hand, attempt a rational de-

* E. A. Nordlinger, *The Working Class Tories*, London, 1967. R. T. McKenzie & A. Silver, *Angels in Marble*, London, 1969.

19

cision in terms of a sober calculation of material advantages: that is, in terms of instrumental values. In contrast, then, to the deferential working class, who are naturally Conservative, and the solidaristic working class, who are naturally Labour, the seculars are not attached to any party but vote according to their assessment of the relative merits of the competing parties. Although McKenzie and Silver claim that the number of secular voters is growing they are still seen primarily as a deviant minority. For the vast majority voting is simply a matter of basic, and largely stable, psychological orientations.

A similar emphasis on psychological orientations can be found in attempts to explain the electoral failure of Labour during the 1950s. Thus we find: '. . . traditional working-class attitudes had been eroded by the steady growth of prosperity', and, 'People who would be objectively classified as working class in terms of occupation and family background have acquired a middle-class income and pattern of consumption and sometimes a middle-class psychology'.*

Such views, which suggest that affluent workers are somehow becoming middle class, and therefore Conservative, have been dignified by critics as the 'theory of embourgoisement', and clearly depend on the assumption that Labour voting is natural for the working class. Conservative voting is again seen as 'deviant', as some sort of aberration: to be explained by the erosion of traditional attitudes or by the acquisition of a middle-class psychology. There is no attempt to explain voting, or changes in voting, in terms of any sort of rational choice.

A somewhat different type of explanation is given by cross-pressure theories.[2] Here different factors, different features of an individual's life situation, are seen as predis-

---

* D. E. Butler & R. Rose, *The British General Election, 1959*, London 1960, p. 2. A. Crosland, *Can Labour Win?* Fabian Tract 324, 1960 p. 13. See also the discussion in D. Lockwood & J. H. Goldthorpe 'Affluence and the British Class Structure', *Sociological Review*, 1963

posing people to vote in different ways. Thus, in Britain, being middle class, having middle-class friends, spouse, or parents, home ownership and so on, lead to Conservative, or non-Labour voting. Being working class, having working-class friends, spouse or parents, being a tenant, belonging to a trade union, and so on, lead to Labour voting. Clearly many people will be influenced by both pro- and anti-Labour factors, e.g. working-class home owners with middle-class friends. In some cases such cross-pressures lead to indecision or non-voting, in other cases of cross-pressure those acting in one direction may predominate. On this view, for example, the high proportion of Labour votes in isolated working-class constituencies is explained in terms of the absence of cross-pressures, of all pressures acting in the same direction. It should be noted that Labour voting as such is not explained here – the pro-Labour pressures on any individual are, in terms of the theory, only overwhelming because there are so few anti-Labour voters around. At most the theory accounts for deviant voting, for the size of the aberrant minority. Here again, then, the theory assumes an automatic relationship between class and voting behaviour.

In spite of their serious weaknesses, which I shall come to shortly, such theories have been widely accepted by students of political behaviour. Even the widespread criticism of the embourgoisement theory has been concerned primarily with the factual question: are affluent workers acquiring a middle-class way of life and psychology? The basic theoretical assumption that working-class psychology means Labour voting and middle-class psychology means non-Labour voting has remained unquestioned.

Such an unquestioned assumption is unfortunate for several reasons. The most obvious of these is that a theory which is based upon the relative stability of voting behaviour is at best able to account for relatively minor changes – which may, of course, have great electoral significance. Such a theory can have nothing to offer in a situation in which the 'natural' relationship between class and voting behaviour appears to break down. By-election results and opinion polls conducted since the 1966 General Election suggest that such a breakdown may be taking place. Mark Abrams[3] in a recent survey showed that forty-seven per cent of those who voted Labour in 1966 did not at present intend to do so again. Changes of this order cannot be treated as minor variations from the established pattern of two-thirds Labour, one-third Tory. Abrams suggests that the defectors, who were largely working class, had 'looked to the advantages which a Labour Government could bring in terms of prices, full employment, social benefits'. The defection is then explained in terms of the failure of the Labour Government to deliver the goods. In other words the defectors are behaving rather like McKenzie's secular voters, but there are too many of them to be treated as a deviant minority.

Whatever the merits of this particular explanation, it is important to recognize that it involves an implicit rejection of the various theories indicated above. This situation suggests either that the above theories no longer apply in the new situation, or that they have never applied. In the first case we need to explain how and why voters' orientations towards politics have changed: why are there suddenly so many secular voters? In the second case the apparent stability of voting behaviour between, say, 1950 and 1966 must be accounted for. In either, the relationship between class and voting, and more generally between class divisions and political divisions, must be brought into question.

I shall argue that the refusal to examine this relationship constitutes a serious and near-fatal weakness of the above theories. The relative stability of voting behaviour on which, as I have noted, these theories are based, is deceptive. The Labour Party of, say, 1950 is not the same thing as the Labour Party of 1966. Nor, of course, have the Conservative or Liberal Parties remained unchanged. In spite of many similiarities, then, a Labour, or Conservative, or Liberal vote in 1950 is a rather different thing from a Labour, or Conservative, or Liberal vote in 1966. Similarly, it could be argued, a Labour vote in Hampstead is a very different thing from a Labour vote in Ebbw Vale. More generally, similar overt activities (voting Labour) in different times and places may have very different meanings for the people concerned (Labour voters). It is unreasonable, then, to assume that the same explanation can be applied.

I do not, of course, intend here to suggest that it is never legitimate to aggregate votes cast, or voting intentions expressed, in different areas. On the contrary, for the purpose of psephology, where the concern is largely with the number of votes or seats obtained by a party, it is entirely reasonable to treat one Labour vote as very much like another. The predictive success of most opinion polls is sufficient evidence of this. However, assumptions which are entirely adequate for the purposes of short-term prediction may be most unreasonable in any attempt to understand long-term changes in political behaviour. In particular, the assumption that one Labour vote is very much like another tends to obscure possible differences and changes in the meaning of these votes for those who cast them.* It will be one of the themes of this book that the dramatic collapse of Labour support after the 1966 General Election must be understood in terms of such long-term changes in the meaning of

---

* At the time of writing the work of Butler and Stokes was not available (D. Butler & D. Stokes, *Political Change in Britain*, London, 1969), but a digest of their conclusions suggests that they take this assumption to an extreme by treating Labour votes over several generations as being basically the same thing ('Labour's Secret Strength', *Sunday Times*, 28 September 1969). 'They [the vast mass of people] take over the family political attitude almost as unconsciously as they take over the family customs about the hours of mealtime or the rituals of mourning.' It is difficult to take this sort of thing seriously: it mistakes the name of an activity (Labour voting) for its content. See also the comments on party loyalty in Chapter Eight.

Labour voting, and more generally in the meaning of politics, among the working class.

If we accept that Labour votes in 1950 and 1966, in Hampstead and in Ebbw Vale, are not entirely equivalent then, at the very least, we should attempt to understand voting behaviour in terms both of differences within the party and of changes in the party over time. Furthermore the meaning, for the voter, of changes within the Labour Party will depend, among other things, on the differences and similarities between it and other parties.

I am not saying simply that we should consider voting behaviour in relation to party policy – although, of course, policy should come into it. There are several reasons for believing that the public claims of the various parties do not determine the meaning a voter gives to his act. A number of studies have shown that a large proportion of party members have no idea, or a false idea, of what the party's policy is on particular issues – and that a large proportion disagree with what appears to be the official policy.[4]

Such apparent ignorance should not be too surprising. It is frequently very difficult for anyone who is not a party spokesman to say what the policy is. Very often political parties do not have a single policy or any particular question. Rather, at any particular time, they have several policies with, at most, a family resemblance between them: the policy expressed in any one statement depending, to a considerable extent, on the context in which the statement is made.[5] What is surprising, then, is not the apparent ignorance of party supporters but the number of researchers who appeared to believe that parties do have policies that can be simply stated; that it was reasonable to ask party members or supporters to say what these policies were and that there was a right answer which the researcher and other political sophisticates knew. In any case, at a time when few people believe that parties will fulfil their pledges, we cannot expect these pledges to have overwhelming importance in voters' assessments.

A more general point is that the relationship between parties and electors is far too complex to be studied simply in terms of party policy and electors' assessment thereof. Abrams and Rose, on the basis of a national survey carried out in 1960, claim that Labour is regarded by a large majority of its adherents as being essentially a class party.* For such supporters, assessment of what they believe to be party policy may depend crucially on the fact that it is proposed by a class party, by a party that is 'more for the working man'. Furthermore, even where such supporters oppose what seems to be party policy, this need not be taken as grounds for opposing the party. Thus assessment of policy often depends on a prior assessment of the party concerned. This prior assessment may depend in turn partly on earlier policy and partly on a large number of other features of the situation.

An hypothetical, but not I think entirely fanciful, example may suggest something of the nature of this complex relationship between party and elector. Suppose that, in what used to be called a safe Labour seat, the party activists can be divided roughly into working-class members, who make up a slight majority, and a substantial minority of shopkeepers, managers, teachers and other professionals, and full-time union officials. Suppose further that, in response to some action of the Labour Government, perhaps some new development of the prices and incomes policy, most of the working-class activists become rather less active – by rejecting the party altogether or by becoming largely inactive supporters.

In this new situation a majority of the activists would come from the previous minority of shopkeepers, teachers, and so on. These members would now dominate the process of selecting candidates for local, and possibly for national, elections. This could have important consequences, over a period of time, for the composition and policy of the Labour group on the local council. In a more immediate

* M. Abrams & R. Rose, *Must Labour Lose*, London, 1960.

sense local councillors and the local M.P. will get their first hand impression of the 'feeling of the party' predominantly from these remaining activists. The change in active membership, then, could well affect the policies and actions of the local party and, if there were similar changes in other constituencies, may have some effects on the parliamentary party. These effects in turn could lead the local or national party into actions which are equally unpopular with the recent activists. This may lead to the increasing dominance of the middle-class groups in the local party, and so on.

I have sketched here a possible course of development which, while it parallels, more or less closely, developments in a number of local Labour Parties, is only one of several possibilities. At each stage there are other possible outcomes: the working-class activists may, for example, stay on and fight within the party. Other sequences may develop out of purely local disputes within the party. Nevertheless it is clear that the development outlined above, and many other possible developments, can involve not only a change in the active membership of the party but may also affect the less active supporters.

Even allowing for the drastic oversimplification of the above example it should be clear that an analysis of political behaviour which attempts to deal with long-term developments necessarily involves an examination of the complex interrelationship of local and national party structures, of M.P.s, party officials, councillors, local activists, inactive supporters, and so on. In particular, change at any of these levels, in any of these groups, has consequences at other levels, in other groups; furthermore these consequences may in turn lead to further changes. Even this is an oversimplification for we need also to take account of other parties, of economic changes (e.g. in the pattern of employment), of urban redevelopment, and so on.

It should not be thought that an analysis of national developments can afford to ignore what appear to be purely

local issues. Thus while the particular housing developments in any one local authority area are unlikely of themselves to have national consequences it is unlikely also that
the local consequences of housing developments in local
authorities throughout the country will cancel each other
out at the national level. The point here is that many
features of British society affect national politics indirectly
through their effects at the local level in many different areas.

More generally I would claim that it is precisely through
the complex interrelationships of the type indicated above
that structural changes within society have their political
consequences. Thus, to take an example to which we shall
return several times, changes in the relative proportion of
public and private housing in the country as a whole do not
have their political effects in any simple and direct fashion.
On the contrary these changes are operative at the level of
the individual family, street, community – that is by
changing the real housing situation of, the real housing
choice open to, large numbers of individuals. At this level
the effects clearly depend on a number of other features
of the individual's situation. Political effects at the national
level (changing patterns of party support, etc.) are the
aggregate results of these, often very different, local effects,
combined perhaps with changes in party images.

Of course many consequences may be observed without
bothering with these complexities; others will be obscured
unless these complexities are examined. However, no account of how changes have come about, or of how stability
has been maintained, can be complete if the above interrelationships are ignored.

I have argued, then, that in order to deal with the long-term
development of political behaviour it is necessary to consider not simply the overt action of large numbers of individuals but also the meanings which these actions have
for the individuals concerned; that similar overt actions may
cover a wide variety of meanings both for those who act

and for those who respond to these actions. Further the meanings of political action, of voting one way or another, for the people concerned must be understood as existing and developing within a complex interrelationship between different levels of the political system, between different types of political action – and all this within a complex and changing environment.

Thus while an analysis of political behaviour must be in terms of the meanings actors give to their behaviour it is not sufficient to remain at the level of the individual actor. We would not, for example, explain the behaviour of U.S. marines in Vietnam simply in terms of what this means for each individual marine – or for that matter in terms of so-called psychological factors such as tough- and tender-mindedness, physical and moral courage or cowardice, obedience, and so on. On the contrary these meanings, these factors, exist and are important only in the context of an already structured situation. In this case the individual marine acts in terms of his situation in a particular military organization which is related in specific ways to other military, political and economic organizations. Explanations of marines' behaviour which remain at the individual level in effect take the war itself for granted.

Similarly political behaviour exists within a structured situation and analysis, if it is not concerned simply with short-term predictions, must be in terms of the complex dialectic of meaning and structure. Thus each individual acts within a social context which, as far as he is concerned, is already structured. Yet the combined effects of the actions of many different individuals may change the context within which each one of them acts – often without anyone intending these changes. Action, in other words, has its meaning within a structured situation and, at the same time, this situation is structured by the actions of people. In the long run neither the structure of the situation nor the meaning which individuals give to their actions can be taken for granted.

The preceding discussion of explanations of political behaviour is by no means exhaustive but it is perhaps sufficient to indicate what, it seems to me, is the major weakness of current analyses; that political behaviour is not normally analyzed in the above terms. Such an analysis would indeed present many problems and, in this book, I attempt nothing more than a preliminary analysis of part of the theoretical area outlined above. The following chapter is concerned with providing a theoretical framework appropriate to the analysis of the interrelationships of party, its members and possible supporters, with particular reference to the working-class members and supporters of Social Democratic Parties. This framework will provide the basis of the later more substantive chapters.

Before moving on to the relationships between party and member it is perhaps worth considering the effects on working-class political activity of what might seem to be non-political factors. It has often been noted, for example, that low income groups, unskilled workers, and those living in areas of low economic status are less likely than others to be politically active or even to vote. A number of studies suggest that political attitudes and mental health are both related to working conditions. Thus Kornhauser* claims that less skilled manual workers are the most likely to have poor mental health while professional and managerial workers are the least likely – and that this appears to result from working conditions rather than from any pre-selection process. For this reason, then, they are likely to be less able to participate effectively in such formal organization as political parties. Similar points may be made with respect to general living conditions. The psychological effects of extreme overcrowding hardly need be mentioned here but there is also a more general argument. Schorr,† for example,

* A. Kornhauser, 'The Mental Health of Factory Workers', *Human Relations*, 1962.
† A. L. Schorr, *Slums and Social Insecurity*, 1964, p. 148.

claims that 'the city dweller, though he may be well off, is not guaranteed his status. To the extent that the city fails to serve him, confuses him, creates stresses for him, it adds an element to those that may set him on the road to poverty.' Those who succumb to such stresses are again less likely than most to participate effectively in political activity.

Such arguments can only apply of course to a minority, albeit a fairly substantial one, of the working class. More generally relevant is the point that the urban working class are less likely than other people to participate in organized voluntary associations. This is not to say that they are less socially active than others – although some may be – but that their social activity is not formally structured. In particular the widespread displacement of primary by secondary groups which is often associated with urbanism appears to be a largely middle-class phenomenon.[6] Since contemporary political parties are, among other things, organized voluntary associations this point has obvious relevance to political activity; directly, since a party is itself a voluntary association; indirectly, since those who are already members of other voluntary associations have a greater opportunity to develop the social skills necessary for effective membership of political parties.

It cannot reasonably be denied that the working classes, particularly the less skilled, less well-paid, sections, are less politically active than other sections of the population. Nevertheless the above explanations of this situation are deceptive in their simplicity. It is by no means clear why the stresses of poorly paid, less skilled work, should lead to a lowering of political activity. The political consequences of such work surely depend on the way it is experienced by the worker; and the experience is not determined solely by the character of the work. 'The strong inclination to resignation in political questions is often conditioned by personal experience' writes Popitz et.al.: 'One cause of this is the daily experience of the work environment which is constantly driving home to the worker that it is not *he*, but "them", the "bosses", who make the decisions.'* But this situation only leads to resignation if it is experienced as unalterable: as it was, for example, in the vast majority of Popitz's sample. If Popitz's workers believed, on the contrary, that this situation was alterable by political action then the psychological and political consequences would be very different. Thus the fact that less skilled, poorly paid workers tend to be politically inactive, politically resigned, is indicative, if only negatively, of what political activity means to them. Similarly the relationship between poor housing conditions and political inactivity exists in part because those living in these conditions do not believe that their own political action can achieve much. Many of the stresses of poor housing depend on this political pessimism. It is interesting in this respect to note that, while the community organizations, tenants' associations and squatters' groups which have developed in many cities in the last few years represent a form of political action, these groups operate to a greater or lesser extent outside the already existing political structures. In particular their actions are not channelled through local Labour Parties. The significance of such developments will be discussed in a later chapter.

The argument in terms of participation in voluntary associations is also deceptive, though for rather different reasons. While British political parties are in many respects similar to other voluntary associations there are crucial differences which are important not only to the sociologists or political scientists but also to those who choose to join or not to join. Most important of these is the fact that a political party is primarily concerned with the acquisition and exercise of political power. It is, in particular, an organization through which members may attempt to exercise some control over the political process. Thus it is interesting, but of no particular importance, if members of certain social groups

* H. Popitz, et. al., *Das Gesellschaftsbild des Arbeiters*, Tubingen, 1957, p. 240.

are less likely than most to join, say, a chess club: but if members of these same social groups are also less active in political parties, this is both interesting and important. The fact that the pattern of membership in a political party is similar to that of other voluntary associations is a characteristic of the parties and of contemporary politics that requires further explanation.

Once again, then, except perhaps in the case of studies concerned with short-term prediction, it is a mistake to think of apparently non-political factors as existing somehow outside politics yet influencing political behaviour in some straightforward fashion. The political effects of such factors exist in and through the way they are experienced by the actors concerned. To some extent the nature of this experience will depend on the meaning that politics has for these actors and this in turn will depend on what political parties are up to. Thus, to return again to the example of poor housing, this may be experienced by its inhabitants as alterable by political action, as alterable primarily by individual action (saving for a deposit, having more children so as to jump the queue, trying to influence corporation officials, the pools and so on), or as something which is unalterable, which just has to be lived with. Others, not inhabitants, may experience it as an eyesore or a danger to public health, which the local authority should do something about, as up to the inhabitants to do something about if they want to, as something you drive through on the way to work, and so on. None of these different ways of experiencing poor housing can be explained simply in terms of physical conditions. Furthermore the psychological effects of physical conditions, crowding etc., will depend, in part, on the meaning of these conditions. It is surely clear that an individual's experience of these conditions cannot be treated as independent of the activities of political parties.

Here, too, it is not sufficient to remain at the level of the individual-actor. The above meanings and experiences also exist and are important within an already structured situation. Thus the analysis of the interrelationship of the party, its members and possible supporters will have to be in terms of the meaning of politics, of what politics is thought to be about, of what is or is not experienced as being a political matter, of the social structuring of the meanings of politics and in particular of the differing meanings of politics for different types of political actors. It will also prove necessary to consider the confrontations of differing meanings of politics, of attempts to define particular topics, issues, activities, as politically relevant or irrelevant, legitimate or illegitimate. If it is the case that political confrontations are sometimes about what is to count as politics then the sociologist or political scientist, who also has to decide on this matter, is involved in a choice which is not purely academic. He is also, however aloof or objective he may feel, choosing sides. My own choice should be entirely clear by the end of this book.

2 The Party of the Working Class?

labour not fulfilling uts vote?

Perhaps the best way of beginning an analysis of the inter-relations of a party, its members and supporters, is with a discussion of Michels' thesis of the Iron Law of Oligarchy: the thesis that 'who says organization says oligarchy'. There is, of course, nothing to prove in the case of an organization that makes no pretence of being democratic. However Social Democratic Parties, and many Trade Unions, do claim to be democratic. If, then, the thesis holds for Social Democratic Parties it must, Michels argued, be taken as holding for all political organizations. Arguing in part from his experience in the S.D.P. (the German Social Democratic Party) before the First World War Michels* claims that:

> ... in the life of modern democratic parties we may observe signs of ... indifference. It is only a minority which participates in party decisions, and sometimes that minority is ludicrously small. The most important resolutions taken by the most democratic of all parties, the Socialist Party, always emanate from a handful of the members. It is true that the renouncement of the exercise of democratic rights is voluntary ...

In a similar vein Weber writes of 'active party members who for the most part merely have the function of acclamation of their leaders'.† Michels gives a number of reasons for this situation: some of these relate to differences between, as he puts it, the leaders and the masses; others are more concerned with structural pressures on the organization.

* R. Michels, *Political Parties*, New York, 1962, p. 86.
† M. Weber, *The Theory of Social and Economic Organisation*, Glencoe, 1964, p. 408.

34

Thus, in comparison with the membership as a whole, the leaders have superior knowledge of the workings of the political system. This is particularly the case if the leaders are full-time politicians but, even if they are not, they are still likely to have a fuller and more direct acquaintance with many features of the political system. Similarly, and partly as a consequence of this situation, they will have greater skill in organizing, making speeches + in fact in all the arts of politics. Furthermore, since they have control of the formal means of communication within the party, they are to some extent able to control the political information at the disposal of the rank-and-file members.

At the same time the masses of the members are more or less incompetent. They are generally less educated and less sophisticated than the leaders and very few of them attend meetings. In addition the masses have a psychological need for leadership. On the latter point Michels is supported by Lipset who argues that the underprivileged rely on strong leadership and do not themselves wish to participate in decision making.

At a more structural level the organization operates within an environment containing large and complex state and industrial organizations and opposing, generally undemocratic, political organizations. In order to operate successfully within this environment the organization needs to be able to reach quick decisions – to call press conferences, issue policy statements, produce election plans, at short notice. Furthermore, in order to ensure credibility with the general public, it is necessary to maintain a reasonable continuity of policy, to limit internal disputes and so on. The party is therefore under pressure to have a full-time leadership, or at least a leadership of full-time politicians, served by a professional bureaucracy and a number of specialist advisors. This, of course, further reinforces the advantages, listed above, of the leaders over the membership. As a result of these factors the leaders will tend to spend most of their time in the company of other leaders, party officials and specialists, leaders of other organizations, and perhaps, academics (economists, industrial relations experts, political scientists and sociologists). This is not the place to examine the effects this has on the work of the privileged academics but, on the leaders themselves, an obvious effect is that they see themselves as professionals, as possessors of a specialized expertise with, whether they admit this or not, more in common with their opposite numbers than with the people they supposedly represent. In the British context both Herbert Morrison and Aneurin Bevan have paid tribute to the power of Parliament to transform socialists, if not to transform society.

Thus the leaders are largely insulated from the views, attitudes, interests, of the mass of their supporters. Even their occasional sorties into the lower reaches of the party do little to alter this situation. The privilege of shaking hands with the leader, of having tea and biscuits in the same room after a meeting, is jealously guarded by local leaders and officials or is meted out as a reward for well-behaved activists.

Finally, according to Michels, Social Democratic Parties, while claiming to work in the interest of their members, in fact pursue the interests of the leaders; and their primary concern is with the retention or acquisition of power within the framework of society as it presently exists. Rank-and-file challenges to the leadership can usually, but not always, be frustrated by one or more of several devices: the use of patronage, or a friendly talk, to buy off the ringleaders; the argument that the challengers are rocking the boat, helping the enemy, and so on; the use of their greater expertise and control of internal communications to suggest that the proposed course of action is unrealistic or positively harmful; and, in some cases to appear to accept the demands and then ignore them. If even these tactics fail and the leadership is overthrown the new leaders will be no less oligarchic.

It is a consequence of this situation that social democratic, or other mass parties, function as mechanisms of social control by restraining, reinterpreting or channelling, the demands of the membership. Whether these demands are revolutionary or not, modern political parties effectively exercise their measure of social control to the extent that they give only partial satisfaction to the demands of their supporters, and that these supporters do not attempt other solutions to their problems.

It is difficult, except in odd details here and there, to deny the force of Michels' description of what appears to be the case, more than fifty years later, in Social Democratic Parties. However, it would be a mistake to confuse the description of this state of affairs with its explanation. Michels himself, as the above account shows, is a victim of this confusion. Considered as explanation Michels' account suffers from serious weaknesses. The most obvious point which has been made against it is that the party would get no support if it did not satisfy the demands of the membership. Lipset, in an introduction to Michels' book, appears to find this point sufficient to transmute the Iron Law of Oligarchy into an Iron Law of Democracy. Such alchemy cannot be taken seriously: it does not follow, as Lipset himself would be among the first to point out, that, say, the Russian Communist Party must be democratic simply because it manages to retain the bulk of its membership. The fact that people remain in a party need not mean that all, or even a majority of their political demands have been satisfied nor that they expect them to be satisfied in the future. The belief that a party will prove an effective instrument for the satisfaction of political demands provides only one of several possible motives for joining the party or for remaining within it.

Nevertheless it is clear that a party must provide for at least some of what the members expect of it. Members are necessary as a source of funds, as a source and proving ground for future M.P.s and councillors, as propagandists and as harvesters of the party vote at election time. Michels provides no satisfactory account of how the party retains its membership while pursuing the interests of the party leaders. Nor is it possible to provide such an account on the basis of an extreme dichotomy between the leaders and the led, the oligarchs and the masses. The rank-and-file membership is not, as Michels too often assumed, either an undifferentiated whole or an unstructured heterogeneity. Even if the party were almost entirely working class, as was the S.D.P. before the First World War, this assumption would not be justified.[1]

In other words we cannot talk in terms of 'the leader' and 'the masses' without introducing elements of mystification and reification into the discussion. It is necessary, rather, to look for the differential pattern of relationships between leaders and led, for differences in political expectation and concern, and for the social structuring of returns and satisfactions to be gained from active party memberships. On the one hand such structuring allows party leaders to develop a differential pattern of response. Thus they may play one section of the membership off against another; they may present what appear to be different policies to different sections of the membership – each being encouraged to believe that it alone is given the 'real' policy, other versions being proposed to keep other sections happy; or different leaders may vicariously represent different sections of the membership and thus, for a time, keep them happy without actually doing anything for them.

On the other hand a party with a wide and diverse membership has no need to keep all of its members happy all of the time. Nor should we suppose that the interests of leaders and members are always incompatible. To the extent that these interests arise out of differing ways of life it is worth noting that the differences here will be far less extreme in some cases than in others. This is particularly clear as far as local leaders are concerned but it is true also of national party leaders. Thus even where local or national leaders are especially concerned to keep in touch with grass-roots opinion – and many of them are so concerned – this activity will keep them in touch with some sections of the membership, and their concerns, and not with others. Often in such discussion the leader will feel that he is talking to people who understand his position, who have the interests of the party as a whole at heart, who are not concerned solely with their own sectional interests. Proposals, complaints or demands emanating from other sections of the membership will be seen as unrealistic, irresponsible, as indicating perhaps a problem of communication.

This aspect of the structured diversity of the membership is possibly the more significant in the long run. The manipulative techniques listed above are not invariably successful and it is, in any case, difficult to treat political leadership as simply a matter of sordid manipulation – although political leaders must be expected to exercise their professional skills from time to time. If the political concerns and interests of party leaders are more compatible with those of some sections of the membership than with others, then conflict between some members and leaders may be seen as reflecting political differences within the membership. From this point of view any long-term trends in the pattern of party membership, and particularly of active membership, are especially significant for they represent changes in those social groups whose interests are effectively represented by the party. Such trends can normally be expected to further strengthen the representation of the favoured sections and to lead to further declines in membership from the less favoured sections.

The above points raise several further problems for Michels' account. In particular, as I have already argued, neither the political interests nor the political incompetence, need for leadership, and so on, of the 'masses' can be treated as somehow given, as not requiring further analysis. Nor, for example, is it sufficient to account for these in terms of reference group theory. Runciman's attempt* to account for the contrast between the large and persistent inequalities in British society and the apparent acquiescence in them by most of the population is couched in such terms. Simply put, his argument is that workers tend to compare their income and standard not so much with those of the middle class as with those of their fellow workers. The social horizons of most people are still very limited, their aspirations do not go very high, their terms of reference are very circumscribed. Hence their feeling of deprivation is much less than the actual difference in standards would suggest.

The descriptive adequacy of such an account can hardly be doubted but it is still necessary to explain why reference groups are so limited, why these comparisons and not others. This is a particularly striking case in which the present structure of politics is especially relevant. Thus it is surely significant that such limited comparisons take place at a time when none of the major political organizations offer any hope of changing the overall pattern of income distribution. Even at the time of Runciman's study the Labour Party was advocating a sort of incomes policy which, apart from a few minor points, took the present pattern of income distribution very much for granted, which specifically emphasized such criteria as comparability and, to some extent, productivity. In such a situation limited comparisons were entirely realistic for, to a large extent, wage negotiations took place in precisely such terms. Wider ranging comparison, particularly if undertaken with a view to political action, would then be entirely unrealistic.

In this case, then, political demands and expectations are formulated in the context of what seems to be politically possible. In the absence of political organizations dedicated to large-scale changes, when in other words there appears to be no prospect of anything but minor changes here and there, it is hardly surprising that people indulge in such

* G. W. Runciman, *Relative Deprivation and Social Justice*, London, 1966.

limited comparisons. On the other hand, of course, political leaders, to some extent at least, act in terms of what they take to be the political attitudes and expectations of their supporters. Party leaders and party members, supporters and opponents all act in terms of a political situation which is already structured and, for each actor, the situation is structured in part by the actions of the others. In particular the apathy, political incompetence, need for leadership of the 'masses' are characteristics, not causes, of the situation Michels is trying to explain.

The problem, then, is to show how a situation with the characteristics described by Michels arises: that is to identify the processes which have led up to this situation. Here Michels' argument concerning structural pressures is clearly relevant. Even a party with a democratic ideology will be under pressure to become oligarchic and further-more, according to Michels, it will succumb. It is worth noting, though, that Michels assumes that the party operates within the institutional environment of western capitalist society, and further that it operates strictly in terms of the established rules and procedures of that society. Thus, at best, his argument shows the impossibility of democratic organization within capitalist society. Even here it applies only to an organization which is not revo-lutionary, or which aims at revolution through parliamen-tary means. It may perhaps be argued that a revolutionary socialist party must also be oligarchic but this would not follow from Michels' thesis. Both assumptions apply to the British Labour Party as well as to the S.P.D. Such parties then, partly in response to environmental pressures (and only because they follow the dominant norms and proced-ures of that environment), change their power structure through the routinization and bureaucratization of their decision-making procedures. These changes do not happen overnight nor are they ever complete. Some decisions remain formally at the local level and, in this respect, the structure of decision making within the party will parallel the structure of national and local government.

For any particular member it is clear that some issues will matter more than others and that decisions relating to such issues will have more importance than other decisions. Furthermore, since the membership is by no means homogeneous, the salience of issues and the criteria by which decisions are assessed will be different for different sections of the membership. I have, for example, already suggested something of the range of political meanings of poor housing. Many party members, for whom public housing is primarily something for others, are likely to see housing policy as primarily a matter for experts to decide within limits set by political and financial constraints; as an economic regulator, a useful deflationary tool. Party members living within poor housing may be expected to see things rather differently: they may not appreciate the overriding importance of keeping rates down or of redeveloping the city centre, they may question the morality of using public housing as an economic regulator.

Of course, the situation is more complex than the above remarks suggest. Nevertheless it should be clear that different sections of the membership may use different criteria to assess particular items of policy: that an account of policy which seems entirely reasonable to some members may make other members very angry and that this is not simply a matter of communication. Furthermore, while many members may be concerned primarily with the broad criteria within which the experts work, others may be very concerned with particular details. Such differences reflect different conceptions of the distinction between political and technical issues, and what is often the same thing, different assessments of the importance of local control.

As a rather different sort of example, consider the question of the selection of candidates for local or national elections. Again decisions taken in this area can be assessed in terms of several different criteria and, oversimplifying considerably, it is possible to distinguish at least two of these. On the one hand, for fairly obvious reasons, it is important for the city or the national party to have some control over candidate selection. On the other hand, for equally obvious reasons, the adoption of candidates is a matter for the local party to decide. There is a built-in source of conflict here but the vast majority of party members will almost certainly accept both criteria. However, for both local party members and party leaders, the relative importance of these criteria depend on the local area concerned. Thus in the case of areas where party candidates have no chance of being elected it makes little or no difference to the character of the party in Parliament or in the local council who is selected. Here candidate selection will not matter much to the national or local leadership. Party members will tend to feel that their selection procedures are free from interference but they will also be rather concerned about the overall character of party representation in Parliament or the local authority: that is they will tend to emphasize the first criterion. Where party candidates have a good chance of being elected the situation is rather different both for party leaders and for local members. The leadership will be more concerned with candidate selection and more likely to interfere while the local members will be on the lookout for such interference and will tend to emphasize the second criterion.

The above situations will be discussed in more detail in later chapters and I have introduced them here primarily for purposes of illustration. Not only are many decisions not bureaucratized and routinized but the importance of such bureaucratization as occurs will vary considerably from one group of members to another and will depend on the specific criteria on which the decisions are based. In particular, some sections of the membership will be concerned to control, or at least influence, particular policy decisions while other sections will feel that such local control is inappropriate in these cases.

Here again, it is a mistake to talk of disputes, or of differences of interest, between the leadership and the membership of the party. Such disputes normally concern only some sections of the active membership; others will view the local demands concerned as unrealistic, irresponsible or even irrational. It is not simply a matter of the power of the leaders or of the rank-and-file, nor is it simply a matter of the appropriate level for decision making. This appropriate level is not simply a feature of the policy area concerned: it depends also on the criteria to be used in making the decision. Thus disputes over the level at which decisions should be taken, over who should take them, often involve different conceptions of the relevant criteria. These conceptions, as the discussion of housing and candidate selection shows, reflect different political concerns, different political interests.

Disputes between members of different levels of the party organization are not simply organizational disputes – although protagonists may express themselves in such terms. Also at stake is the question of which political interests, which political orientations are to provide the criteria for policy making.

Hence, as far as effects on the rank-and-file are concerned, it is not the fact of oligarchy, or the process of becoming oligarchic that matters, but the specific organizational form that the oligarchic party takes and the greater or lesser extent to which this form of organization is compatible with the interests and concerns of different sections of the party membership. Changes in organizational structure may well reflect changes in the interests predominantly represented by the party. Such changes, of course, will be related to changes in the pattern of active membership within the party. Here it is necessary to consider the position of various factions within the party and of the many Left groupings outside it. Such factions and groupings provide a training ground for local activists, and sometimes for local and national leaders, but they also provide a refuge for many discontented activists. Changes in the relationship between the party and other Left groupings may also be related to changes in the pattern of active membership within the party.* The above changes may also, in the long run, be related to changes in electoral support through, for example, the decline of locally known activists who would otherwise function at election time as vote collectors.

It is hardly necessary here to argue that, in broad terms, Michels' account is at least as relevant to the analysis of the contemporary Labour Party as it was to the continental socialist parties of the early 1900s.[2] Indeed, if the above points are born in mind then a suitably modified form of Michels' argument is relevant not only to the analysis of how the party becomes oligarchic but, far more generally, to the discussion of changes in the membership, structure and activity of an already oligarchic party.

It is in this sense that Michels' work provides a framework for the analysis of the interdependence of party power structure, the pattern of party membership and support, and party activity. In the following chapters I will attempt to apply this framework to the development of the Labour Party since the war with particular reference to the changing position of the party's working-class members and supporters. Thus my primary concern will be with the analysis of the changing structure of the grass-roots party organization.

Since, as the above discussion suggests, changes at this level do not take place without a struggle we shall expect such changes to occur gradually in some cases and dramatically, following the outcome of some local battle, in others.

* The relationships between the various Left groupings, the Communist Party and the Labour Party have not been the subject of systematic study and the most recent study of the Communist Party hardly mentions other groups (K. Newton, *The Sociology of British Communism*, London, 1969). I am in no position to remedy this situation and, although I do comment on such relationships from time to time, the absence of any systematic analysis of this area constitutes one of the more serious gaps in the present work.

Particularly important in determining the outcome is the support given to one side or another by the national or regional party organization. Such an analysis must therefore be concerned with other levels of the party organization and, more generally, with political, economic and other structural changes in British society.

In particular the generally oligarchic nature of contemporary political parties will be taken for granted in what follows and I will not be concerned, as Michels so obviously was, either to demonstrate or to condemn the undemocratic nature of social democratic parties. That political parties are more or less undemocratic has long since been taken for granted by most serious students of politics. This point is not, in itself, of any particular significance for the future development of democratic societies. Far more important in this respect is the fact that fairly substantial sections of the population are becoming increasingly isolated from, and poorly served by, the present political system. The consequences of this situation will be discussed later but it should be remembered that such isolation cannot be explained solely in terms of the present characteristics of the isolated.

3   The City Party I

As a political unit the large or medium sized city has two particularly important sets of characteristics. On the one hand the city is administered by one local authority which, in physical terms at least, is not remote from its inhabitants. In this respect the city is similar to other county boroughs and very different from, say, a small town which will be administered by at least two local authorities, at least one of which is likely to be some distance from the town itself. Political parties in the city are organized on three levels: the ward; the constituency; and the city itself. The city party, because of its size and the relative ease of communication, will be fairly well organized and will often employ one or more full-time officials. The whole local authority area is the battleground for both inter-party and intra-party power struggles. Again, partly because of the relative ease of communication, the party group, or caucus, on the city council is often fairly coherent and fairly well organized. Since both the city party and the party caucus are fairly well organized and concerned with all local authority matters, opportunities for conflict between them are relatively frequent. In particular for rank-and-file party members opportunities for obtaining information about and, at the very least, for attempting to exert control over, any or all local authority issues are greater in the city or county borough than in most other areas.

On the other hand the large or medium sized city contains, in a relatively small area, a large population living and working under a very wide range of conditions with a relatively high degree of residential segregation between the different levels of wealth and poverty. Small cities and other communities contain neither such a range of conditions nor such a degree of residential segregation. Indeed many county boroughs are very largely single class communities: either middle- or working-class residential suburbs with or without an attached industrial estate, or more isolated single-industry communities. The city thus contains a number of more or less distinct communities, some of which are fairly homogeneous, each with its own set of political interests and concerns. This situation is reflected within the major political parties and more particularly within the Labour Party.

Thus political conflict within the party relates not only to ideology or to national policy but also to the different problems faced by different groups and areas in the city. Even where members in different areas express concern over the same substantive problems there are differences in their perceptions of the importance or urgency of the problem and particularly of what would count as a reasonable solution. The sources of potential conflict are therefore numerous. However, if the city party is to survive and to achieve any degree of electoral success these conflicts need to be contained and, if possible, neutralized. The processes to be described in this and the following chapters may be seen in part as resulting from attempts to meet this need or at least from actions which are presented in such terms. I do not, of course, intend here to suggest that it is somehow the party as such which makes such attempts. On the contrary, various individuals and sections within the party will have rather different conceptions of what changes are necessary to meet this need. It will be argued that, to the extent that members of some section or sections have succeeded in imposing their own conceptions of the needs of the party, this has led to a change in the structure and character of the party itself.

It is perhaps worth emphasizing that differences between areas should not be seen as influencing politics from outside. In the case of housing conditions, for example, I have already argued that it is not the physical conditions as such that are politically significant but the political meaning which these conditions have for various political actors. Even the conditions themselves are not independent of political action. Indeed the growth of planning in recent years suggests that the evolution of modern cities is increasingly based on political decisions. Such decisions do not in the first instance relate to the best way of doing this or that: they are part of the more general division of limited financial and other resources. It is, as Labour propaganda would no doubt have it, a question of priorities. In other words these decisions are based on the realities of political and economic power. The distribution of power, in both senses, throughout the community is therefore of particular importance in determining the future shape of present cities – and, for example, non-participation in the formal political process results in, and may result from, the absence of such power.

This is not, of course, to deny that there are many purely technical problems involved in the planning of redevelopment. The point rather is that the range of possible solutions is limited by political and economic considerations and by the criteria which are, so to speak, taken for granted by those involved in the specification or solution of planning problems. Of particular interest are those cases where the decision is thought to be a purely technical one, for this can only occur where the values and criteria involved in defining the problem and limiting the range of possible decisions are taken for granted, are part of the commonsense world of those able to influence such decision making.

I have already argued that participation in the formal process of politics is related to environmental conditions. Thus urban structure not only poses problems for the urban planner but it also indirectly affects the availability of resources for their solution – if indeed any is to be attempted. The relationship between politics and urban structure, then is by no means one-sided.

The remainder of this chapter will be concerned primarily with the political structure and ecology of the city as it appeared in the mid-1960s – that is before the magnificent post-1966 collapse of Labour support. Following a brief discussion of urban structure I shall introduce a fourfold classification of city wards. The following sections will consider the distribution of party membership, active membership, councillors residing in or representing a ward, over these four types of area. These sections are primarily descriptive and much of the data is presented in the form of tables – although I have tried to keep these to a minimum.* A brief summary will conclude this chapter. The data here presented provides a basis for the examination of the political concerns and political interests of ward parties in different areas and some of the relationships between these parties. This in turn leads on to the discussion of the extent to which the grass-roots structure of the party has changed since the war and to an attempt to account for such changes. In particular I shall attempt to place the later collapse of Labour support in the context of longer term developments in working-class political involvement.

Housing and Population Structure

The work of the Chicago school of urban sociologists[1] provides the basis of a preliminary classification of the types of living conditions and the forms of residential segregation existing within the large or medium city. We may begin, then, with Burgess's broad differentiation of the city into four cultural zones outside of the commercial and financial

* The discussion in this and the following two chapters uses evidence drawn largely from a study of the Liverpool Labour Party in 1964-1965. Tables 3.1 and 3.2 are based on data from all 40 wards in the city while the remaining tables are based on a sample of nine wards. The precise figures should not be taken too seriously for reasons discussed at length in Chapter Five.

districts of the city centre: a zone of transition; a zone of working-class homes; a middle-class residential zone; and a commuters' zone. It makes little difference, for the purpose of this study, whether these zones are viewed as concentric rings or simply as areas which are more or less physically distinct.

A brief examination of the development of cities should suggest something of the physical character of these zones and of the relationships between them. The beginnings of the segregation of residential areas according to position in relation to factories, warehouses, civic buildings, drainage and prevailing winds appeared in the growing industrial settlements of nineteenth-century Britain and, somewhat earlier, in the great commercial ports and a few other centres. On the one hand one had the homes of the upper middle class: the captains of industry in Manchester and Birmingham, the merchants and brokers (of slaves, tobacco, cotton) in Bristol and Liverpool, all with good access to central facilities and, as far as possible, avoiding the dirt of the factories or the smell of the docks and warehouses. On the other hand one had the rows of working-class homes built near the factories or docks, in the marshy land at the bottom of the hills, or for the more skilled and respectable, on the slope of the hill below the mansions of the upper middle class. Between the two were the homes of the growing white-collar groups: shopkeepers (the high-class provision merchants), professional and supervisory employees.

The homes of these three groups provide the characteristic buildings of what is now the inner ring of the city – the transitional zone. The great urban overflow of the twentieth century, whereby many of the original inhabitants of these areas or their descendants have moved out to more desirable conditions has left these types of housing to pass on to other residential or commercial uses. Hence the development of the transition zone as a distinctive area is clearly linked to the growth of upper middle-, and other middle-, class suburbs and the somewhat later growth of areas of cheaper private-enterprise homes and of publicly owned working-class suburbs.

To some extent these later developments, particularly the growth of council housing, represent the growth of the political and economic power of the urban working class and lower middle class. In some cases the early development of public housing may be seen as resulting from the exercise of political power by the organized working class while in many other cases such developments appear to have resulted from defensive or preventive measures carried out by the locally dominant middle class. In either case, however, two points are crucial: substantial sections of the working class did not benefit from such developments; the principal mechanism for the exercise of local political power by the working class was the Labour Party. On the latter point it is clear that, at best, the exercise of working-class power over the housing market depends on working-class control over the local Labour Party. It will be argued later that local Labour Parties are becoming increasingly less effective as mechanisms of working-class control over the housing market. While, in a situation where the Welfare State is more or less accepted by all parties, this may not affect the quantity of public housing provided to any great extent, it may well affect the forms that such provision takes and the nature of what is provided. I shall return to this point later.

On the former point it is clear that these newer forms of housing are considered both desirable and normal in the city and that, to some extent, those of the working class who remain behind are in an increasingly disadvantaged position. In particular these groups suffer from the competition of a middle-class minority of romantics and intellectuals, relatively unsuccessful criminals, students and other deviants, and of course various immigrant groups: furthermore the remaining inhabitants of these central areas often become stigmatized simply by virtue of living there.

However it would be a mistake to close the analysis of

urban zoning at this point. The transition zone in particular is an ever-changing area. The population itself is continually changing as public rehousing continues and, deviants and many immigrants apart, the inhabitants tend to view their situation as a transitional one – mistaken though many of them may be. This zone furthermore is perpetually under attack along its inner boundaries and loses ground to financial, commercial or industrial areas, while at the same time it tends to expand beyond its outer edges. Of more recent significance, perhaps, is the fact that it is the transition zone which suffers most heavily from the building of urban motorways and the geometric growth of car-parking facilities around the inner core. Finally, and to an increasing extent, rehousing takes place within the old transition zone itself with the old high-density housing being replaced by new, and only slightly lower density, housing.

At the same time it should be noted that public housing has now been in existence for several generations and that public housing estates vary considerably in both quality and reputation. In part this results from the constraints put upon public housing by various governments but an increasing number of estates appear to be designed specifically for the lower income and status groups – for the stigmatized residents of the transition zone. A number of local authorities have also developed the policy of isolating awkward tenants by bringing them together into one estate.

Thus, while it may once have been true that working-class suburbs were more desirable areas than the older transition zone, it is certainly no longer the case that all public housing estates are considered as desirable and normal places to live, even by those who can afford nothing else. This is particularly so for much of the housing that is replacing the classical transition zone.

Thus the situation in contemporary cities is more complex than the fourfold division of Burgess and the Chicago school would suggest. As far as this study is concerned the situation is even more complex, for the basic units of political organization are local election wards and a number of wards cut across the boundaries between two or more zones. The rather rough classification of wards which follows necessarily obscures many important differences but it shares with the Burgess model the merit of simplifying the subsequent discussion. The primary purpose of my classification is to simplify the presentation of data while taking account of at least some of the more important differences between areas – differences which are neglected here will, of course, be brought into the text wherever necessary.

For the purposes of this classification it is convenient to divide the population into four socio-economic categories:

A – professional and managerial workers;
B – clerical and other non-manual workers;
C – skilled and self-employed workers;
D – semi- and unskilled workers and those in personal service.

Using these categories it is a simple matter to classify the city wards according to the relative proportion of the above groups in the population. Thus[2]:

1 – wards with a higher than average proportion of both middle-class groups (A and B);
2 – wards with a higher than average proportion of lower middle- and skilled working-class groups (B and C);
3 – wards with a higher than average proportion of both working-class groups (C and D);
4 – wards with a higher than average proportion of the semi- and unskilled groups only (D).

This classification corresponds roughly to what is intended when we speak of middle-class areas, working-class areas and so on, but even wards in the first category contain, at the very least, a substantial working-class minority if not an actual majority. Although their bases are rather different the above classification corresponds fairly well to that developed by Burgess and his associates. The fuller description given below should make this clear.

1. Middle-Class Wards

These areas are generally safely non-Labour even though they frequently contain a majority of manual workers. Population density, number of persons per room and number of households per dwelling[3] are all low – housing is only a problem if there is a danger of rates being increased in order to finance it. Streets and air are clean, street lighting, education and other facilities (often including parks) are good and refuse-collection is relatively efficient. There is little noise from traffic except in exceptional cases.

2. Lower Middle- and Skilled Working-Class Wards

These are generally politically marginal wards – but marginal with a non-Labour bias. The population density, number of persons per room, and number of households per dwelling are generally a little lower than average. Housing is not much of a problem. The streets and air are a little less clean, lighting and education facilities are still reasonably good, as is refuse-collection. There may be some council houses and, very occasionally, a few council flats.

3. 'Respectable' Working-Class Wards

These are more or less safe Labour areas.* Population density and number of persons per room are generally rather higher than the city average and a number of wards have a high rate of households per dwelling. These wards tend to belong to the inner zone of working-class homes bordering on the zone of transition, or to the outer working-class estates. There are therefore many council homes but

* This comment refers to the period between the late 1940s and the early or middle 1960s. There are now no safe Labour areas in the cities.

still relatively few council flats. The outer wards in this group have relatively clean air and streets and relatively little traffic noise. The others do not have these advantages. Street lighting, education facilities, and so on are less good and refuse-collection is less efficient than it might be.

4. Less 'Respectable' Working-Class Wards

These also are more or less safe Labour areas. Population density is high, except where residential areas are interspersed with factories, warehouses and so on. The number of persons per room is also high and there is often a high rate of households per dwelling. These wards belong mainly to the classical transition zone or to the areas of council housing, mostly flats, which have invaded this zone. There are also, however, a few of the less respectable outer working-class estates in this category. Except in the latter case, and sometimes even there, the air and the street are dirty and there is a lot of traffic noise. Street lighting is generally poor as are the local educational facilities and refuse-collection is often appalling. Repairs to the council housing in this category seem to take longer than in the more respectable areas.

Most of the characteristics listed above will not be referred to in the detailed analysis which follows and the broad characterization is intended mainly as a background against which the details should be seen. There is however one notable exception, and it will be seen that the differences in housing conditions are of particular significance – perhaps simply because housing is the most striking feature of the overall superiority or inferiority of particular areas.

It is perhaps worth noting that overall turnout in both local and national elections is now substantially lower in the working-class areas than it is in the other two areas. The differences in this respect are often much greater than they were in the early or middle fifties. The significance of this change will be examined later.

Party Membership

It is not an easy matter to discover the precise membership of the Labour Party in many parts of the city. The membership lists, where these exist, are often unreliable. They contain the names of people who are dead, have long since left the area, are no longer members and, in extreme cases, do not even know that they are in the party.* Estimates based on affiliation fees paid by the ward or the constituency party are also, for reasons which will be discussed more fully later, unreliable. The party constitution generally allows any person who has paid at least one month's subscription in the current year to be a member. Thus membership, according to this minimal definition, may cover the whole range from, at one extreme, someone who has been contacted once in the heat of a membership drive and has no further contact with the party, to, at the other extreme, a member who spends every free moment working for the party. In particular, differences in membership between wards may indicate simply that someone is prepared to go round collecting subs in one case and that no one is prepared to do this in the other.

Not only is it difficult, then, to trust figures of party membership but it is not at all clear what membership differences mean, however well established they may be. In a sense, then, active membership (those who attend meetings, collect subs, canvass) is a more meaningful indicator of party size than is total membership. Nevertheless, while it is difficult to make much of differences between one ward and another, differences which appear fairly regularly between one type of ward and another cannot be accounted for by purely random factors. It suggests perhaps that activists in one type of area have difficulty in recruiting members or that they have no interest in doing so.

Bearing in mind, then, that their precise significance will

* Where, for example, a husband 'joins' his wife without her knowledge.

have to be examined later consider the following membership averages:

Table 3.1

middle-class wards	141·6
lower middle- and skilled working-class wards	134·6
'respectable' working-class wards	92·6
other working-class wards	86·0

These figures conceal a considerable range of membership. The lowest admitted membership, twenty-five was
found twice: once in the middle-class category and once in
the less 'respectable' working-class category. The highest,
over 500, was found in the lower middle- and skilled
working-class category. Nevertheless the relationship between membership and type of area is unmistakeable:
membership tends to be smaller in those wards with a high
proportion of manual workers and higher in areas with a
low proportion of these groups.

It does not follow from these results that the membership
of the party is largely middle class, for approximately half
the population in the most middle-class wards come from
the working class. Nevertheless even if we accept, as is still
probably the case, that a majority of the membership is
working class it is significant that out of a total city membership of about 4,700 the two types of working-class wards,
with about half of the city's population, supplied only about
1,500 – less than one-third.

As far as active membership is concerned, I have again
taken a minimal definition: an active member is one who
attends ward meetings more or less regularly. Thus, while
there may well be more active members than attend any
particular meeting, I do not expect there to be many more.
If ward A regularly has more people at its meetings than
ward B then it has a larger active membership. I have,
therefore, taken the average size of ward meetings as an
indication of the number of activists. Since a majority of

wards in the less skilled working-class category did not meet more than once or twice a year I have, for purposes of presentation, combined the two working-class categories in much of what follows. Since 1965, when this data was collected, a number of other wards in the working-class areas have ceased to meet regularly.

For those wards still holding regular meetings average attendance (over the year) was as follows:

Table 3.2

middle-class wards	12·6
lower middle- and skilled working-class wards	12·1
working-class wards	10·6

Here again the relationship between active party membership and type of area is unmistakeable. In view of the earlier discussion of developments within the transition zone it is worth noting that wards which have long had a high proportion of council flats have the lowest membership and attendance rates in the city. In wards containing newer blocks of flats, again largely in the old transition zone, there were no members, at the time of the survey, from these blocks. The consequences of this type of rehousing thus appear to have been disastrous as far as Labour's grassroots organization is concerned.

The above tables refer only to the overall numbers of members or of active members. They tell us nothing about the members or active members themselves. In an attempt to remedy this situation as far as active membership is concerned I have analysed those attending meetings in a sample of nine wards: three each from the middle-class and lower middle-/skilled working-class areas and those from the two more working-class areas. Since I have, of necessity, considered only wards which hold meetings I have, if anything, overestimated the amount of activity sustained by the working-class areas.

Table 3.3

PARTY ACTIVISTS: by Ward and Socio-Economic Group (%)

	Profes-sional	Manag-erial	Skilled	Non-manual	Semi-	Un-skilled	N
Middle-class areas							
Population	6·5	16·2	34·0	24·2	11·4	7·7	
Officials	56·0	22·0	11·0	0	11·0	0	9
Activists	44·1	20·6	20·6	8·8	5·9	0	39
Lower middle-/skilled working-class areas							
Population	0·7	4·7	41·2	14·8	20·9	17·7	
Officials	43·0	14·3	14·3	14·3	14·3	0	7
Activists	13·6	9·1	41·0	13·6	22·7	0	22
Working-class areas							
Population	1·2	4·1	38·2	10·9	20·6	25·0	
Officials	33·3	16·7	0	33·3	16·7	0	6
Activists	35·8	7·2	28·6	21·4	7·2	0	14

Table 3.3* compares the occupational characteristics of ward officials (chairman, secretary, treasurer), active members and of the population at large, in different types of area. Comparing the activists with the general population it is clear that the less skilled groups are consistently under-represented – but more so in the more working-class areas. There were no unskilled workers attending meetings in any of the wards studied. Skilled workers are also under-represented, albeit to a lesser extent, except in the lower middle-/skilled working-class areas. Professional and managerial groups are over-represented in all wards while the remaining non-manual groups are most strongly represented in the most working-class areas and least represented in the middle-class areas.

Professional workers are in all cases the most significantly over-represented category among party activists but it

* The occupational classification here follows that used in the 1961 census reports.

should be noted that this category includes a wide range of occupation. The five 'professionals' in the working-class wards consist of two full-time union officials, two teachers and a social worker. At the other extreme there are, out of fourteen 'professionals', one union official, four teachers and no social workers.

Considering the activists alone, without reference to population, the party is most working class in the lower middle-/skilled working-class areas, and most middle class in the more middle-class wards. There are, however, more working-class activists in the most middle-class areas (nine) than in the most working-class areas (five).

The listing of ward officials is probably rather misleading since there are too few of them to give a reliable picture. It is, nevertheless, worth noting how few manual workers are ward officials.

Table 3.4

PARTY ACTIVISTS: by Socio-Economic Group (%)

	Profes-sional	Manag-erial	Skilled	Non-manual	Semi-	Un-skilled
Population	2·3	7·5	36·5	16·1	18·9	19·0
Officials	43·1	17·4	8·2	19·1	14·2	0
Activists	30·8	12·6	30·2	14·1	12·3	0

The above results allow for an approximate estimate* of the representation of various occupational groups in the city Labour Party as a whole (table 3.4). It is clear that all categories of manual workers are under-represented, the skilled workers least of all, while the professionals are the most over-represented. In terms of the overall number of activists, the city Labour Party is primarily that of the skilled manual and professional categories with semi-skilled, managerial and other non-manual minorities. Thus,

---

* This estimate is derived from Table 3.3 above by weighting each group of wards by the total number of activists in the group. It should be taken as, at best, a first approximation.

while on the basis of its active membership, it is difficult to talk of Labour as 'the party of the working class' it would be a mistake to go to the other extreme and treat it as very largely middle class. In 1965 at least, the city party still had a substantial minority of working-class activists. However, it will be seen later that the political concerns of the ward parties appear to relate more to the location of the ward within the city than to the class basis of its membership. Political conflict within the party cannot then be explained simply in terms of class differences.

Party Councillors and Aldermen

It is already well established that local councillors, of any party, tend to be of a higher socio-economic status than either their constituents or the rank-and-file members of political parties – and that this is particularly so for the Labour Party.[4] The working-class groups in particular are poorly represented in all parties, but rather less so in the Labour Party than in others, and of all working-class groups the unskilled are the least represented. In any area where there is a fairly high degree of residential segregation between classes this has the consequence that, in the Labour Party, many council members belong to a ward party in one type of area and represent a ward in another – this would not, however, apply to any great extent in the Conservative or Liberal Parties.

Table 3.5

COUNCIL MEMBERS BELONGING TO WARD PARTIES

Type of Ward	*Number of Council Members*	
	High	Low
Middle-class area	6	3
Lower middle-/skilled working-class area	2	10
Working-class area	3	12

Table 3.6

ATTENDANCE OF LABOUR COUNCILLORS AT
MEETINGS OF WARDS THEY REPRESENT

Type of Ward	Attendance at Ward Meetings	
	Regular	Irregular
Lower middle-/ skilled working-class area	9	2
Working-class area	6	9

This point is brought out clearly in tables 3.5 and 3.6. In the first of these, wards have been divided into those with more than the average number of council members and those with less. Those working-class wards with a higher than average number of council members are all largely council estates and many of these councillors represent the area in which they live. Table 3.6 covers wards represented by at least one Labour councillor and wards have been classified according to the extent to which these councillors (or one of them) attend meetings of the ward party. It will be shown below that active membership is closely related to both the number of resident council members and to the attendance of local representatives at ward meetings.

Table 3.7

STATUS OF COUNCIL MEMBERS
BELONGING TO WARD PARTIES

Type of Ward	Number of Chairmanships, etc.	
	High	Low
Middle-class areas	8	1
Lower middle-/skilled working-class areas	2	10
Working-class areas	2	13

Table 3.7 considers the geographical distribution of high status Labour council members – those who are chairmen or deputy chairmen of important committees and so on. It is clear that in this respect, also, there is a strong bias in favour of the middle-class areas and comparison with table

3.5 shows that this cannot be explained simply in terms of the high number of councillors living in these areas. Council members living in the more working-class areas are likely to be of lower status.

The sample of party activists showed a similar bias in favour of middle-class areas as far as prospective candidates were concerned. Thus we find:

middle-class wards: four councillors, four prospective council candidates, three prospective parliamentary candidates;

lower middle-/skilled
working-class wards: one councillor, one prospective council candidate;

working-class wards: two councillors only.

It is worth noting that the two latter councillors both represent the ward – largely a corporation housing estate – of which they are members. A similar pattern would, of course, be found if we examined the geographical distribution of officers of the city and the various constituency parties, but it is hardly necessary to do this here.

Table 3.8

ACTIVE MEMBERSHIP AND COUNCIL MEMBERS
BELONGING TO WARD PARTIES

Active Membership	*Number of Council Members*	
	High	*Low*
High	6	3
Medium	4	13
Low	1	9

Table 3.9

ACTIVE MEMBERSHIP AND ATTENDANCE OF
COUNCILLORS REPRESENTING WARD

Active Membership	*Attendance at Ward Meetings*	
	Regular	*Irregular*
High	4	0
Medium	10	6
Low	2	5

The democratic ideology of the Labour Party encourages councillors to take an active part in ward politics – at least by attending meetings of the ward to which they belong. Thus councillors frequently attend meetings of these wards and less frequently attend those in wards which they represent. It seems likely, then, that councillors will play very different roles in these two situations – it will be seen in the next chapter that this is indeed the case. In the first situation, for example, council members or even those who have recently been members, possess both the information and the experience necessary to ensure that the discussion takes place on a realistic plane. At the same time they are in a position to see that complaints and queries are suitably presented to the right quarter and often to ensure that some action is taken – if only in the form of a letter explaining why nothing can be done.

To some extent, of course, a councillor can also play such a role in a ward which he represents. In such cases, however, even when the councillor does attend, his position is likely to be very different from that in the ward of which he is a member.

Thus, it is not too surprising if tables 3.8 and 3.9 show that active membership is associated both with the number of resident councillors and with the attendance of local representatives at ward meetings. Nor is it surprising that this relationship is stronger in the case of resident council members.

Summary

A fourfold classification of city wards has been introduced in terms of housing and population characteristics. With some modification this corresponds very roughly with Burgess's division of the city into the zone of transition, the zone of working men's homes, the middle-class residential zone and the commuters' zone.

In terms of this classification it has been shown that at least in the mid-1960s, both membership and active membership of the Labour Party were related to the type of ward – so that the more middle-class areas were likely to have a higher membership than most other areas. Areas of council houses also tend to have a higher active membership than average but the reverse was the case for areas with a large number of council flats – whether these were newly built or long established. Wards with a high number of households per dwelling have a larger active membership than others of the same general type. This is perhaps attributable to the high proportions of single adult males and of small families in these areas.

The number of council members (councillors or aldermen) who are members of the ward party was also shown to depend on the type of area. Where council members were also members of ward parties in the more working-class areas they tended to live in council estates and to represent the areas in which they lived. This association between number of councillors and type of area was even more marked in the case of relatively high-status councillors. Many Labour council members therefore found themselves representing one type of area and belonging to a ward party in a different type of area – those who represented the area in which they lived tended not to be among the leaders of the Labour Group on the local council.

Active membership of ward parties was strongly associated with the number of resident council members. In those wards which were represented by Labour councillors active membership was associated, though far less strongly, with the attendance of these councillors at ward meetings. It will be argued that, to some extent, these differences are related to the differing roles which councillors play in ward meetings. In both cases, though, the presence of a council member seems likely to enhance the effectiveness, in some sense, of the ward party. This point will be developed in the following chapter but it is clear that this effectiveness will depend in part on the particular demands made by party members in different areas.

In general, little distinction was made between different types of working-class area but differences between the two types of ward tended to be in the same direction as other area-related differences. Wards with a particularly high proportion of the semi- or unskilled working-class groups in the population had fewer active, or inactive members and were less likely to have regular ward meetings. Since the time of this study the organizational weakness of the Labour Party in these areas has increased and has extended to the more respectable working-class wards.

If membership, or active membership, were simply a matter of social class – the total membership depending only on the proportion of various classes in the local population – then the strongest ward parties would be those in the most working-class areas. This is obviously not the case and, as the sample of activists showed, the middle classes, particularly the professional groups, probably provided a slight majority of the city party's active membership. This being the case it seems clear that most published pictures of the party membership by social class are misleading. Furthermore, the fact that ward parties in the middle-class areas had the highest number of working-class members tend seriously to contradict cross-pressure and embourgoisement theories.

4 The City Party II – Political Differences

It has been argued above that political conflict within the city party is not simply a matter of ideology – although this may affect the terms in which disputes are conducted. Nor is such conflict simply a local reflection of policy dispute at a national level. While ideology and national policy often come into local disputes it would be a mistake to ignore the different problems faced by different groups and areas within the city. This chapter will be concerned primarily with an examination of the political concerns and interests of ward parties in different areas of the city, and with some of the relationships between these different parties.

I am not here concerned with whether people agree or disagree with party policy or even with whether they know what it is. Some of the difficulties involved in the use of such questions were discussed in Chapter One: in particular that the policy expressed in any particular statement depends on the context in which the statement is made and is, in any case, intended as much to make an impression as to indicate what the party is actually going to do. The confusion that exists as to what party policy is, even among active members, is hardly surprising for it is, to a large extent, fostered by the parties themselves.

A rather different problem with this type of question is that its use usually involves the researcher in a decision as to what is, or is not, politically significant – and more generally as to what counts as political. Thus, for example, attempts to measure 'knowledge of party policy' involve a number of policy areas which are thought, by the researcher, to be politically important. Similarly questions intended to measure 'knowledge of politics'[1] involve the researcher in a decision as to which political facts it is most important for people to know.

Since, as will appear shortly, the concerns of some party members would be dismissed by other members as not political, it is difficult to assert with any confidence that some political issue or fact is more important than some other. Of course, in the capacity of political actor, we all make such decisions but we are not thereby justified in stigmatizing those who decide differently as politically ignorant or irrational. I have already suggested that such stigmatization is itself a political act, but it is also one which can effectively cloud our understanding of political processes.

For these reasons I have avoided any attempt simply to compare reactions to what I consider to be politically significant issues. To some extent, of course, the political concerns of party activists speak for themselves: in argument, debate, discussion. I have therefore used an analysis of topics discussed in ward meetings as a crude indicator of the political concerns of ward parties. However members differ not only in the substantive areas of their concerns (housing, education, roads, etc.) but also in their perception of what the specific problems are, and of what would count as a reasonable solution. Thus an examination of political concerns involves an analysis both of topics discussed and of what is not normally discussed, of what is implicit, taken for granted, in normal discussion. Confrontation between councillors representing a ward and ward members are particularly revealing in this respect: the points at which communication breaks down, or at which tempers get lost, often indicate that what for one person is obviously important is, for another person, irrelevant.

In the following discussion, then, the tables listing topics discussed and the time spent on them in different types of area are not intended to measure differences – except in the very crudest sense. It will be seen, for example, that fifty per cent of the time in working-class areas is devoted to housing while in the middle-class wards less than five per cent of the time is spent on this.

This does not mean that housing is therefore ten times more important in one area than in another: it is, in any case, not at all clear what could be meant by such a numerical comparison. There are, among other things, very great differences as to what is important about housing.

The tables are intended rather as a very crude indicator of differences and as a focus for the subsequent discussion of political concerns and of the meanings of politics. Numerical data of this sort should always be used with great care.

As a preliminary classification we may broadly divide political concerns into those relating to policy and those relating to party organization although there will, of course, be some degree of overlap between these two areas. These broad areas of concern will be discussed separately although, as this broad distinction is not entirely satisfactory, the discussion in both cases will range rather more generally.

In all cases something in the region of sixty to seventy per cent of time in ward meetings was spent on discussion of party organization or of procedural matters. This, it has often been argued, is one of the major reasons for poor attendance at party meetings.[2] Such an explanation does not seem particularly adequate and, if anything, it is the larger parties, in more middle-class areas, that spend most time on these matters. Furthermore, the category of party organization does not, as will be shown below, include only items which are intrinsically boring or uninteresting. Politics, whatever else it may be, is to do with power and its exercise, and the distribution of power within the organization may be of particular concern to some of its members.

Policy Concerns

Policy concerns may be dealt with in two ways: according to the topic itself or according to whether the concern is with ward, city or national questions. In both respects there are important differences between ward parties.

Table 4.1

POLICY TOPICS DISCUSSED

Policy Topics (% *time spent*)	Middle class	Type of Ward Lower middle/ skilled working class	Working class
Housing	4	28	50
Education	14	4	10
Traffic control	17	36	2
Amenities: local	6	2	6
Amenities: city	11	1	0
Corporation activity	1	20	28
National economy	8	5	6
Foreign policies	17	0	0
Immigration	24	0	0

The headings used in table 4.1* are, I hope, largely self-explanatory. Traffic control includes provision of crossings, parking facilities, control of speed and flow of traffic; amenities include things like parks, footpaths, libraries, shopping facilities, play streets, etc., and local amenities are those relating specifically to the local, ward population; finally, corporation activity covers a large number of small items relating to actual or desired activity of the city corporation and not covered under any of the other headings.

* Here, and in subsequent tables in this chapter, percentages add up to more than 100. This is because, in several cases, it was impossible to place a discussion in one category only. All figures refer to the period 1964–5, as does most of the discussion, although the present tense is frequently used in order to avoid awkwardness in the presentation.

It is clear that, even at this very crude level, there are some very pronounced differences in the policy concerns of the various ward parties. One of the most striking, if not particularly surprising, of these relates to housing. This, as earlier chapters have suggested, is worth discussing in some detail for differences in the political meaning of housing are intimately related to many other differences between areas.*

In the middle-class areas, housing, as a topic for political discussion, was primarily something to do with other people, with people who 'perhaps through no fault of their own' were unable to make adequate provision for themselves. The provision of housing was a political priority, a social responsibility. About this there was no question, although the exact position of housing in the overall hierarchy of priorities was unclear. Thus there could be dispute over whether or not the building industry should be included in the general economic squeeze, over the relative weight in economic policy to be given to public as opposed to private housing, over the extent to which the local authority housing account should be subsidized from the general rate. On this latter question it would be pointed out that council tenants pay rates as well, and that a large increase in rates would be politically disastrous. Often, it seemed, activists thought that a really good direct-works department would make all the difference and would, furthermore, be a good example of socialism in practice.

The lack of attention to housing at party meetings in these areas did not, then, indicate that party activists did not consider it important. It was rather an indication of the way in which activists perceived housing as a policy issue. While the broad outlines of housing policy were a matter for political decision, the execution of policy within these broad outlines was primarily a matter for experts. At a national and at a local level what was needed was a general

---

* For an alternative view of the political significance of housing see J. Rex and R. Moore op cit. Some of the differences between the two approaches will be discussed in a later chapter.

policy which was both humane and fair but, above all, a really good team of planners and architects in the relevant corporation departments and some proper co-ordination between the planning and the housing department. Apart from this, private landlords should be controlled and, if necessary, their property should be subject to compulsory purchase.

Thus little attention was given to housing because, it was felt, this was not an area in which laymen had much to offer. Given the broad outlines, corporation policy would be judged in terms of its efficiency in providing a public service. Activists, in these middle-class wards, believe their approach to housing is both rational and humane and feel hurt that other activists often appear not to appreciate their position – if, as is the case with councillors or ex-councillors, they ever come into contact with activists from other areas.

It should be pointed out, however, that in these areas housing has another very different, more personal, meaning which is not experienced as political but which is, nevertheless, intimately related to more overt political concerns. Housing, in this more personal sense, is judged not simply in terms of its physical characteristics but also in terms of the sort of area it is in. Thus, in choosing a house, people are also choosing an area with a certain character, with certain amenities and, very often, with certain educational opportunities available locally for their children.

This feeling of choice of area is, of course, often illusory, for the credit system normally gives building societies a degree of bureaucratic control which, together with geographical clustering of home prices, may severely limit the choice available at a given income level. Nevertheless, even where choice is restricted the individual concerned will not normally be aware either of the nature or the extent of the constraints. His feeling of having chosen both house and area will in any case be fully supported by other inhabitants.

Underlying such choice, illusory or not, are various

environmental features which appear, for example, in the language of estate agents or in private, non-political discussion. Such features include: good local schools; somewhere for the kids to play which is relatively free from traffic; secluded but only ten minutes from the city centre; convenient for trains and buses; smokeless zone: bordering on the Green Belt; and so on. Many of these features depend on the actions of the local authority either directly (education) or less directly (smokeless zone, relative freedom from traffic).

Those who have made their choice have a right, so they believe, to expect that the various desirable features of the environment will be preserved or even improved upon. Thus they have an interest in the general urban environment and in civic amenities, and this interest often extends far beyond the immediate neighbourhood – covering, in particular, access to the city centre and the amenities there provided.

The local authority, then, is experienced as providing a background of services and amenities against which housing choice may be made. The home itself is the proverbial Englishman's castle and he accepts responsibility for its upkeep, repairs, and so on. In this respect the Labour activist differs little from his more Conservative neighbours. Where he does differ, as far as local authority action is concerned, is in his view of its responsibility to provide for the less fortunate.

In the more working-class area the situation is very different. To begin with, only a very small minority have any experience of choice of housing in the sense described above and few are able to anticipate having such a choice in the not too distant future. Those who have such a choice or who can confidently expect it (junior academics or young professional couples) are likely to judge housing policy in much the same way as their colleagues in the middle-class areas but to give it perhaps a greater priority.

For the rest such choices are not available. Those who are

offered council housing on the basis of need, length of residence, and so on, are normally given at most two, three or four choices. Often the first home offered will be taken for fear that the later offers will be worse. The choice of housing, if and when it becomes available, will in any event be severely limited. Furthermore, the increasing invasion of the more central areas by redevelopment, urban motorways, wholesale clearance and so on, means that many of those who have no great wish to move will have no choice in the matter.

Those who have yet to be rehoused will often have relatives, friends or at least acquaintances who have moved out to new estates or point blocks or other areas of purpose-built council housing. Not all of these will have moved into the more desirable estates and many will have been deeply unhappy after the move. Those who remain behind, then, can be expected to have some acquaintance, if only at second hand, with the corporation's rehousing policy and to have ambivalent feelings about the possibility of a council house or flat for themselves. On the one hand the chance of better physical conditions may be very attractive – at least to those who do not fall victim to a clearance order. On the other hand they will be familiar enough with different types of council housing to be deeply suspicious of the schemes of the corporation's planners and architects.[3]

In any event, those who experience such limited choice of housing do not judge housing policy in terms of relatively abstract criteria of efficiency – although fairness is extremely important. Public housing is no longer something which is primarily to do with other people nor is it something that can be safely left to the experts to work out within very broad policy criteria.

Here the details matter: why knock down the good homes on one side of the street and leave the bad housing on the other?; why rehouse all but two families in this street and leave the two for months with houses falling down on either side of them?; why haven't the corporation mended the roof of this house which they took over nine months ago?; and so on.*

In all but the most middle-class wards, housing was discussed in terms both of broad policy and of specific details: the former predominating slightly in the lower middle-/skilled working-class areas, the latter in the more working-class areas. Here, at least for many members, it was impossible to maintain the extreme dichotomy between the political and the personal meanings of housing. The scope for misunderstanding was therefore considerable for, even in the most depressed areas, several activists and the local councillor not only could maintain, but insisted upon maintaining, such dichotomy.

Thus for the councillors and for several activists the sort of detailed problems listed above were not the sort of things you discussed in ward party meetings; they were not really political. At best they were individual cases which the councillor would look into, but there was nothing to discuss about them. Often, however, discussion would be insisted upon and, in such cases, an attempt would be made to show how the situation in question fitted in to the overall plan of, say, the housing or the planning department. Since the councillor himself would often not fully understand this overall plan, his account would be rather simplified and would be intended to give the impression that this was not really a matter for laymen.

All too often such an account appears patronizing and furthermore it misses the point. The problem here is not simply that of a lack of communication. Such lack is a consequence of two very different modes of experiencing politics. On the one hand politics is a matter of broad policy outlines, of general principles, and thereafter is a matter of getting suitably qualified personnel and the right sort of machinery to execute policy – hence, for example, the growing emphasis on professional city management, or

* A glance at the correspondence files of provincial evening papers should provide numerous examples of such questions.

76

on training courses for local councillors. This emphasis on broad principles and professional execution corresponds to the experience of local or national government as providing a background, an environment within which individuals may operate. There is a sharp distinction between political and personal matters. Within this general orientation the differences between Labour and Conservative or Liberal activists relates to the type and extent of general background services, or environmental interference, and to questions of efficiency.

On the other hand, local government is experienced not simply as providing a background but also as an external constraining and coercive organization. In particular, questions of housing – which are a personal matter to many of the middle classes, and to some of the working class – are here experienced as something which will be decided by the local authority. In many cases, of course, the results of such decisions may be entirely satisfactory for the individuals concerned but in many other cases they will not. Dissatisfaction with housing decisions, or concern over what the decision in one's own case may be, is widespread. For many others local authority interference is experienced as an ever-present possibility – compare this with the sense of outrage felt by 'ratepayers' at local authority interference in what they believe to be personal matters.

It is the sense of unavoidable personal involvement (actual or potential) in the consequences of political decision that corresponds to the emphasis on the details of policy execution as a political matter – or as something which ought to be political. Many of the working class, and some sections of the lower middle class, have attempted to use their collective power, as organized through the local Labour Party, to control or influence the detailed execution of policy, to obtain for themselves some measure of the housing choice, and all that goes with it, enjoyed by the middle classes. The present weakness of the Labour organization in the working-class areas of cities is a measure of the failure of these attempts. The growth of tenants' associations or community organizations, which attempt to exert local control over housing in what used to be solid Labour areas, is a further indication of this failure. Why, if this is not so, do they no longer attempt to exert such control through the local Labour Party?

The contrast here is perhaps a little overdrawn for there are all sorts of intermediate positions, yet it should be clear that the increasing professionalization of politics, at national and local levels, represents a real loss of effective power by some sections of the community. At the same time the significance of the increasing centralization of politics depends on the modes of political experience of the people concerned: if politics provides background amenities, centralization may lead to improvement in the service offered or to a decrease in costs; where politics is experienced as being closer to home, increasing centralization may be experienced as a loss of freedom.

The contrast is not, in any case, simply a matter of housing,* nor is housing an issue whose significance can be considered as independent of other issues. I have already suggested that the choice of housing carries with it the feeling of all sorts of rights in connection with services and amenities provided by local and national government.† The absence of such choice carries with it not so much the absence of rights but rather rights which are less absolute, more fragile, pertaining to inferior services and amenities. I

---

* A similar contrast in the meanings of politics may be found in the area of economic policy. It is an indication of the social distance between Labour Party and T.U. leaders and their rank-and-file that the leaders are unable to appreciate the nature of this contrast. The fact that the more working-class wards hardly discuss economic policy is also significant in this respect – for it suggests that many of the economic concerns of the working class can no longer be expressed through the formal machinery of politics.

† It is not the fact of having exercised such choice that matters. What matters is that such choice is experienced as being open to one now or in the near future. Several private tenants in the middle-class areas appear to feel this way – often with no apparent justification.

do not of course wish to suggest any necessary connexion here. The point rather is that these are the political meanings of housing and of housing choice in this society. The forms of political organization of housing tend to preserve these meanings.

It should not be supposed that the emphasis on broad principles and professional execution in the middle-class areas somehow prevents the activists from discussing details of policy execution – particularly where these relate to what they experience as their rights. Particular cases, however, are generally discussed as particular cases of general principles or in terms of the interests of the community as a whole. In cases relating to the home neighbourhood it is possible also to argue in terms of the electoral advantages to the Labour Party of doing something about this or that. The topics discussed in this way include things like the provision of zebra crossings, painting yellow lines along the edge of a busy road, and so on.

Since such issues are discussed in terms either of party advantage or of general principles it is an easy matter to present complaints or requests for action in terms appropriate to the bureaucratic rationality of corporation officials or the political rationality of suitably placed councillors or aldermen. Given the nature of their complaints and requests, and the consequent low cost of doing something about them, their chances of getting some sort of satisfaction are relatively high. Even in the case of a high cost area such as education, the costs of maintaining or improving an already good school will generally be less than the costs of radically improving a bad one. In those cases where no effective action is achieved, the form and presentation of their complaints is usually sufficient to ensure at least a polite response – a letter, say, explaining why nothing can be done.

An intermediate, and somewhat anomolous, position is occupied by activists in the lower middle-/skilled working-class areas. They are either tenants of good private housing or of higher status council housing or they are owner-occupiers of older, generally less expensive, property. The latter, however much choice they may have experienced in acquiring their homes, now have a severely restricted choice for they have been left behind in the great increase of property values since the war. They are, therefore, in a very weak position as far as the further exercise of housing choice is concerned. Thus these groups tend to be in a housing situation which is better than average for the city but their situation in the housing market, their ability to exercise choice, is severely restricted. Here again there is the emphasis on the background amenities and services that goes with a relatively privileged housing situation, but the lack of choice in these areas leads to a particular emphasis on the quality of neighbourhood or ward amenities and services. It is not surprising, then, that it was ward parties in this type of area that showed most concern with purely local issues.

Table 4.2

POLICY TOPICS: by scope of concern

Scope of Concern (% time spent)	Type of Ward		
	Middle class	Lower middle/ skilled working class	Working class
Ward	23	57	48
City	46	41	57
National	51	5	11

Finally, in the more working-class areas, activists were in one or other of two positions: either housing choice was effectively open to them (or would be shortly) or they had little or no such choice. There were very few in the intermediate position indicated above. Discussion was often marred by a serious lack of communications which frustrated and annoyed all concerned. Specific complaints or requests were often discussed in ways which brought into question the bureaucratic rationality of corporation officials or which were tangential to the political rationality of the local councillor – who was often prepared to look into particular cases but saw no particular point in talking about them. Furthermore, many of their complaints or requests involved high cost issues. The chances of getting some sort of satisfaction, then, was often relatively low. Where no effective action was achieved the form and presentation of their complaints was rarely sufficient to ensure a polite response and generally received none at all.

Thus, although discussion was often concerned with very specific issues, it tended not to be orientated to specific actions which could be taken by the local councillor or by the local authority. The problem here is not so much that discussion is vague and imprecise (although it often is) but that it does not take a form appropriate to the rationality of the relevant decision-making body. The rationality implicit in such discussion is not the institutionalized rationality of the middle classes, and it therefore appears as irrationality to other activists and to party officials. The charge that officials or councillors are patronizing is thus often justified, however vehemently it may be denied.

In these areas, then, dissatisfaction is likely to be widespread both with the party and with the local authority. To many members the bureacratic rationality of corporation officials appears as highly irrational or as deliberately confusing. Discussions were often characterized by a diffuse and generalized dissatisfaction, a general suspicion and an ambivalent attitude towards the party's representatives on the council. The atmosphere at such meetings is hardly likely to encourage new members to become more active in the party. Those councillors who do not have great difficulty in communicating with the activists in these areas are likely, instead, to have such difficulties in relation to their colleagues on the council. Their position will be discussed below.

Party Organization Concerns

Table 4.3

PARTY ORGANIZATION TOPICS

Organization Topics (% time spent)	Type of Ward		
	Middle class	Lower middle/ skilled working class	Working class
Social	8	11	2
Political education	7	1	9
Premises	2	30	2
Delegates	12	0	0
Relations with city party	14	0	18
Party democracy	0	23	13
Finance	40	21	37
Elections	27	22	34

Here again, I think, the headings are largely self-explanatory and, as far as these topics are concerned, several differences relate simply to differences in the situation of the ward organizations. Thus the long discussion of premises in two wards results from the fact that both own their meeting places – which were inherited from a time when the local party was stronger and financially more secure. One ward was discussing the proposed sale of its premises. As far as the selection of delegates was concerned only the larger parties have the luxury of choice. For the others it is not a question of choice but of trying to find someone.

'Party Democracy' is perhaps less clear than the other headings. Like corporation activity in the previous section it covers a number of relatively small items: small, that is, in terms of time spent on them. However, these items have in common a discontent with the decision-making structure of the party. In all but the middle-class wards there were allegations that undue pressure was being, or had been, brought to bear on the ward, its members or representatives, or that higher officials or bodies within the party had been unfair. Thus, for example, there were complaints that the whip system among the Labour group was being operated in such a way as to prevent representatives of a ward from raising certain issues; that a member of the ward had not been approved as a possible candidate for local elections because he had strongly criticized the policy of the Labour group and, so it was said, because he was working class; that pressure had been put on a ward to adopt a particular candidate; and so on. Such claims would, of course, be denied by party officials or, perhaps, it would be said that the decisions complained of were reached in strict accordance with constitutional procedure. While it is difficult to pass judgement on many of these allegations it is equally difficult to accept all the denials.

Such claims and counterclaims are only to be expected in the atmosphere of general suspicion current in the more working-class areas and, to a lesser extent, in the lower middle-/skilled working-class areas. The appeal to the constitution is hardly likely to improve matters here for this is sufficiently complex as to make it often unworkable. Thus it is not at all unusual for local party meetings to be unconstitutional in one way or another and it is often possible, therefore, for decisions taken at such meetings to be challenged.* For this reason, paradoxically, party constitutions are particularly important for they can be very useful and effective weapons in the hands of those who are most familiar with them. Almost invariably this will favour the full-time officials and leaders, who are already in a fairly powerful position, or, in the case of local disputes, the more middle-class as against the more working-class sections of the party.

It is worth noting also that, in all modern democratic parties, among the most important decisions taken at the lower levels of the party organization are those relating to the adoption of candidates.⁴ Certainly when they involve safe or winnable seats these decisions are of particular

* This point is discussed further in Chapter Five.

concern to higher levels of the organization and, for that matter, to parties in safely non-Labour areas. Hence it is on the local parties in safe or marginal areas, if at all, that pressure is likely to be put. The lack of concern with problems of party democracy in the more middle-class areas is hardly surprising nor is the fairly great concern in all other areas.

The position of local councillors or aldermen is also related to activists' concern, or lack of it, with the decision-making structure of the party. At one extreme, in the middle class wards, council members who are present at meetings are likely to be members of the ward. It is wards in these areas which are most likely to have councillors as party members and these councillors are more likely than those in others areas to have a high status in the council chamber (table 3.5, 3.7). These councillors are encouraged by the democratic ideology of the party to take an active part in ward politics. In this situation council members, or those who have recently been members, possess the information and experience necessary to ensure that discussion takes place on a 'realistic' plane, they can point out what are feasible alternatives, and so on.

Nevertheless, these council members will be present simply as members of the party, and will participate in much the same way as other ward members – with, naturally enough, more relevant information than the others about many issues. Thus party activists in these areas have a good chance of acquiring some familiarity with local authority matters. Furthermore, as a result of more or less friendly discussion with councillors, they may participate indirectly in the formulation of policy. It is activists with such contacts who are most likely to be co-opted on to party or even local authority committees.

In the more working-class areas of the city on the other hand, where attending councillors are more likely to represent the ward than to be members, the situation is usually very different. Activists in these areas will tend, when a councillor is in attendance, to focus many of their requests, complaints, demands upon him. These demands and questions will often be experienced as unrealistic, irrational or irresponsible. He will thus often be forced into the position of defending, or making excuses for, himself and his colleagues rather than of giving information or explanations to ward members.

It is clear, of course, that whether one accepts demands or proposed solutions as being realistic or not depends, among other things, on how seriously one takes the problems concerned and on whether these problems are recognized as being political problems. Since, even in the mid-1960s when the party organization was stronger in working-class areas than it is now, only about one-third of party activists lived in the areas of acute housing problems, and a far smaller proportion of the local leadership lived in these areas, it was not these people who could determine the criteria of political realism. Not only were the active members in other areas, and also the vast majority of local councillors, concerned with a number of other problems, but they were also generally cushioned by a total lack of experience of the severity of the housing situation. Furthermore their experience of housing as a political issue, however important they acknowledged it to be, would be very different from that of many many activists in the working-class areas.

Thus very few councillors are likely now, or were likely then, to accept the criteria of realism implied by the concerns and demands of ward parties in the most working-class areas. Many, indeed, will have great difficulty in understanding these demands at all. Those who do will be considered by their colleagues, in the Labour and other parties, to be unrealistic, irresponsible, extreme. If they are any good at making speeches they may be seen as demagogues.

Councillors from the lower middle-/skilled working-class areas often find themselves in a similar, though less isolated position, for it is in these areas that local men are most likely to be selected as candidates. There are thought to be sound electoral reasons for such choices, for anything that will add to the appeal of a Labour candidate in a marginal ward is important. Councillors who both represent and live in a particular ward are, then, particularly likely to come from this sort of area, or from larger council estates. In either case their position in the local party is often such that their colleagues see them as being too concerned with purely local matters, as narrow rather than extreme.

If such councillors, narrow or extreme, wish to move into more powerful positions within the Labour group they must demonstrate that they have acquired the right sort of realism or the appropriate breadth of concern. This may well be seen by many rank-and-file members as 'selling out'. Yet those who are sufficiently self-conscious to be aware of the change may consider that they have no real alternative. In any case there will be substantial social support for this new realism.

Thus, to a large extent, Labour councillors are supplied, and both confirmed and supported in their realism, by ward parties whose concerns and characteristics are very different from those in the areas these councillors represent. In particular many councillors feel, quite correctly, that they are 'in touch' with the feelings of the rank-and-file. At the same time some sections of the rank-and-file feel that these same councillors are 'out of touch' and treat them accordingly. Those who provide such treatment can only be perceived as, at best, unrealistic by those who receive it. At worst they are seen as ungrateful, narrow minded, but 'what can you expect when they're forced to put up with conditions like that.'

For many activists in the working-class areas and often for those in the lower middle-/skilled working-class areas the concern with party democracy is not simply a result of pressure, or of any specific complaint. Underlying such complaints is the more general feeling that they are somehow losing control of the party, that it doesn't seem like 'their party' any more. This feeling appears, for example, in their suspicion of, and ambivalence towards, these councillors and the party hierarchy, and in their exaggeration of the glories of the past. Those councillors who are thought to be 'all right', to be 'good' councillors, are often very isolated in the council chamber. In such cases the suspicion of, and ambivalence towards, the party hierarchy is particularly marked.

At the other extreme, underlying the lack of concern with party democracy in the middle-class areas, is the generally unacknowledged feeling that, in spite perhaps of many policy disagreements, this is their party. Both types of feeling, acknowledged or not, are reasonably accurate. These feelings furthermore are continually reinforced, in both cases, by their experience of the party, by discussions of policy or party organization, within the ward or with party officials.

It is time now to discuss the way this situation has come about.

5   The City Party III – Change

The political differences discussed in the previous chapter suggest that different types of member have very different experiences of the party. In particular, party meetings in the more middle-class areas are more likely to attract new members and to retain older members than are meetings in other areas. It is tempting, then, to explain changes in the pattern of party membership in terms of such different experiences. If anything, we would expect a tendency for the party to grow in the middle-class areas and to decline more or less quickly elsewhere. However, this sort of explanation applies only after the process of growth and decline has set in, for it presupposes that the party is dominated by the middle-class areas. It is necessary, also, to account for this dominance. This explanation of change based on the present experiences of party members accounts perhaps for the continuance, but not for the origin, of this process.

The remainder of this chapter will be concerned primarily with an examination of those changes in the pattern of party membership which have led up to the general situation described above. It is difficult, however, to make any precise assessment of changes over time, for records are not always reliable and are often non-existence. Nevertheless it is still possible to make an estimate of the extent and direction of changes in membership, or at least in active membership, by examining the present activists and their various, often contradictory, memories. Before doing so it is perhaps necessary to discuss the reasons for the lack of reliability of party membership records. These reasons are themselves of some political significance.

The Reliability of Records

In the course of a dispute with her local constituency party Mrs Braddock, M.P. for Liverpool Exchange, complained to the N.E.C. of the Labour Party that the membership returns of the Exchange constituency party were inaccurate. The membership was, she claimed, shown as 1,273 at the 1953 annual conference, as 1,635 in a return to the regional party organization in March 1954, and as 633 at the annual meeting of the local party in the same month. Her own opinion was that the membership was 'not above 400'.[1] In reply, the chairman of the constituency party claimed that the first two returns were calculated on the basis of membership cards bought over the year and represented consecutive years, while the third was based on returns from ward secretaries and represented current membership. The constituency party was reorganized by the N.E.C. and a membership return of 677 was given for the following year.

It is difficult to know what to make of such figures. On the one hand the returns based on annual sales of membership cards could be taken as representing some 'real' membership. In this case the Exchange constituency party gained 252 members during 1953, thus continuing its steady growth since the end of the war, and lost almost two-thirds of its membership in the following two years. But what are we to make of the 1,000 or so 1953 members who had either not rejoined or had not been contacted by March of the following year. On the other hand the relatively high returns could be taken as representing 'real' membership and hidden donations in unknown proportions. The much lower return of 1955 may, then, represent a similar sort of mixture with different proportions or even, for the party was then short of funds, an underestimate of the 'real' membership.

However these figures are interpreted it is clear that there was some change in the Exchange party between 1953 and 1955 and that the reorganization of the party by the N.E.C. may have had something to do with it. What is not clear is the extent to which this represents a significant change in the membership of the party. Furthermore, as will be seen below, the differing interpretations on this point have a political significance. There are no politically neutral figures who can reveal the 'true' situation.

It is difficult, then, to trust the membership returns for individual constituencies given in the Annual Conference Reports until 1957. Nor is there any good reason for placing greater trust in figures for the total individual membership of the party which are still given in conference reports. The 1957 Annual Conference, for example, decided on a new minimum affiliation fee based on 800 members per constituency. By the following conference the National Agent was able to announce an increase of nearly 70,000 in individual membership most of which, it seems, occurred in the smaller constituency parties. Again it is not at all clear what this apparent change represents.

Such membership totals are calculated on the basis of affiliation fees paid by, or membership cards bought by, constituency parties. At the same time ward and constituency parties send delegates to other bodies in accordance with their total membership – with, of course, a minimum number of delegates so that even the smallest of the formally constituted parties may be represented.

Thus, in calculating their membership return, ward or constituency parties act under the influence of two conflicting considerations. On the one hand the more members a ward or constituency claims the more it has to pay out. On the other, the fewer members a party claims the less its representation on other bodies. In the case of ward parties the relative strength of these considerations will depend on the position, financial and otherwise, of the ward. Thus, for example, a ward party with largely working-class activists in an otherwise middle-class constituency may, if it is not too short of money, be concerned to overestimate its actual membership. In other circumstances a ward may be concerned to save as much money as possible. In some cases ward activists rely on those who are delegated to the constituency from, say, their union branch to 'represent' the ward. The Fabian Society, the local Co-op, and various professional associations (Socialist Teachers, etc.) may be similarly used in other areas. Clearly the eventual membership total must bear some relation to the number of paid-up members – a ward party with twenty-five members could hardly pay up for 500. Nevertheless there is still considerable room for manoeuvre.

Pressures of a rather different sort operate at other levels of the party organization. In particular, full-time agents and other paid officials of local or regional party organization are under pressure to increase, or at least prevent a decrease in, the membership in their area – or to appear to do so. Membership totals are further complicated by the existence of Labour Clubs in some areas but not in others – for membership of the party is often a condition of membership of the club. Many such clubs appear to have been run primarily in order to finance party activity and having therefore spent too little in maintaining the premises which have become progressively more shabby and less comfortable. In these cases the provision of new recreational facilities in the area may lead to a rapid decline in party membership.

A further problem is that membership claims are sometimes subject to political dispute. A close decision at a constituency meeting may lead some of those on the losing side to question the credentials of the delegates present. Since not all of those who attend ward meetings are eligible to be members of that ward – because they no longer live in the ward or even the constituency – residence qualifications are frequently questioned. When this fails, the right of the delegating body to appoint so many delegates may also be disputed. In such cases constituency, city or regional party officials may find it convenient to discover a decline in membership in some areas.

It would be naïve to assume that these various pressures somehow cancel each other out in the calculation of the membership totals published in conference reports. There is no obvious interpretation of fluctuations in published membership. In a sense then, as I suggested in Chapter Three, active membership (those who attend meetings, collect subs, canvass, and so on) is a more meaningful indicator of party size than is total membership. Here again, however, records – in minute books and so on – are hardly reliable and, in many cases, are missing or contain no record of attendance. At one ward meeting which I attended as an observer I was somehow counted twice and added to the six members present to make a quorum of eight – but only after I was asked if I had any objection to this procedure. In a number of other cases, ward parties which met only twice a year (once to re-elect ward officers and once to select a candidate) had very well-produced minutes of a further eight meetings.

In this case also, the apparent objectivity of numerical records cannot be trusted. It is necessary, then, to rely on memories of members, ex-members, officials and so on, to attempt to make some sense out of their often contradictory versions of past events.

A Preliminary Estimate of Change

A preliminary estimate of changes in active membership, can be made on the basis of the age and length of membership of present activists.* There are, of course, obvious dangers in basing projections into the past on present data and it is clear that estimates obtained in this way provide at best for very tentative conclusions. Such estimates do however provide a check, albeit an imperfect one, on the

* The data here is based on the sample of wards reported in Chapter Three.

various accounts of the past which will be considered in the following section.

Table 5.1

AGE AND LENGTH OF MEMBERSHIP

Type of Ward	*Age* (*variance*)	*Membership* (*variance*)
Middle-class area	43·6 (133·1)	13·9 (159·2)
Lower middle-/ skilled working-class area	50·4 (14·3)	19·8 (76·2)
Working-class area	46·5 (234·1)	21·6 (325·0)

Table 5.1 gives the average age and average length of membership of activists for different types of ward party. The figures for the variance of these factors give a rough measure of the distribution of ages and lengths of membership around these averages.

The lower middle-/skilled working-class areas are perhaps the most exceptional: the members had the highest average age and a high average length of membership; and in both cases, particularly age, there is much less variation than in the other areas. In these areas the Labour Party activists were almost all in their forties and fifties and few of them had been in the party either a very long or a very short time.

Elsewhere the situation was very different. The middle-class areas show the lowest average age and by far the lowest average length of membership. More significantly, perhaps, there were active members of all ages and lengths of membership – including a few who had been members since the party started and a few who had only just joined. The more working-class areas had the highest average length of membership and an intermediate average age. The high variance figures indicate some old, some middle-aged, and some young active members with few in the intermediate age groups. Similarly for length of membership: the active members had been in the party since it started, since the immediate post-war years, or for only one, two or three years.

In the absence of drastic changes in the last few years such data gives a picture of party membership over a longish period of time. The lower middle-/skilled working-class areas had very few new active members – only two members, out of a total of twenty-two, had joined the party in the past three years; the middle-class areas had the highest proportion of new active members – nine, out of thirty-four, had joined in the past three years – and a fairly continuous range of lengths of membership; finally the working-class areas also had a fairly high proportion of new active members – four out of fourteen – but no continuous range of length of membership.

It would seem, then, that new members were becoming active in both the middle-class and the working-class areas, but only in the former case did many of them remain active. Few new members became active in the lower middle-/skilled working-class areas. At the other extreme, the more working-class areas had a high proportion of members who had been in the party for a very long time, the middle-class areas had fewer of these and the remaining intermediate areas fewer still. One does not need the help of actuarial tables to see that such data gives the following pictures:

middle-class areas – continuous recruitment of new active members, many of whom remain active in the party; this, together with the relatively continuous range and low average length of membership, suggests a slowly growing number of activists;
lower middle-/skilled working-class areas – very few new active members, a large proportion of activists who joined in the late 1940s, and a few longer-term activists; this suggests a slowly declining, or at best static, active membership;
working-class areas – continuous recruitment of new active members few of whom remain active within the party (at least in these wards), most other active members joined either in the late 1940s or much earlier; this also suggests a declining active membership.

In particular, then, the data suggests that wards in all but the middle class areas have at one time had a larger active membership than the figures in Chapter Three indicate – although, of course, there may be individual exceptions. This should be particularly the case in the two more working-class types of area. In fact, at the time of the survey, almost half of the wards in these areas did not meet, except perhaps for the ward committees to re-elect themselves, and all of them claim to have met regularly in the past.

Thus there appears to have been a marked shift in membership since the war from the more working-class to the more middle-class areas of the city. It would, however, be a mistake to interpret this simply as a shift from working-class to middle-class membership for, as table 3.3 shows, there is a substantial minority of working-class activists in the middle-class areas. Nevertheless, this shift may indicate that class, in the strict socio-economic sense of the term, has become of less importance as far as activity in the formal political structure is concerned. This question will be the subject of a later discussion.

Myths and Memories of the Past

The tentative conclusions listed above were often, but by no means always, supported by the testimony of ward secretaries. It is not possible, however, on the basis of such data, to assess at all accurately when the process of growth or of decay had set in or how rapidly it had occurred in the past. Unfortunately changes in the number of activists in local parties are hardly news and it is rare indeed for such changes to reach the columns of the national, or even local, press except perhaps incidentally in connection with local scandals or with large-scale internal battles. The biographies or autobiographies of political figures operate on a more elevated level and rarely notice grass-roots events – except perhaps in the early days of our hero. Academic studies of politics are similarly lacking in information concerning the rank-and-file of the parties except perhaps at one point in time in one place. In these various sources, also, it is possible to find incidental mention of changes in the number of activists in connection with internal battles. For example, in the joint autobiography of Jack and Bessie Braddock we find that their final defeat of an unholy alliance of 'revolutionary Communists, members of the Co-operative Party and Bevanites' in the Liverpool Exchange constituency party led to the disbanding and reforming of the party without 'the Communist and Trotskyist elements'.[2] If the figures published in Annual Conference Reports could be believed there were almost 1,000 such undesirables in this one constituency party in 1953 (i.e. about two-thirds of the membership'.

In this area, unfortunately, such highly coloured accounts, more or less detailed memories, myths and stories, are all one has to go on. Naturally various accounts contradict one another but it is possible to identify a number of types of history or myth current within the Labour Party.

The term myth is not used here in any derogatory sense. It is intended rather to emphasize a number of features of such accounts.[3] In particular there is no justification for taking any one account as historically accurate (although one may be) and measuring the others against it. Furthermore such political accounts serve not only to convey information but also to support a particular world view, a set of political attitudes and assumptions which are more or less taken for granted, in terms of which facts and events have their political meaning. Memories of political events are revised in their recounting in accordance with changes in one's own position, the extent to which one knows or trusts one's audience, the impression one wishes to leave, and so on. In this respect political memories are no more reliable than any others. Similar points apply to the first-hand, or other, stories and accounts. In all cases such myths and stories are as interesting for what they reveal as for the facts they purport to convey.

These accounts may relate to specific events, as in the case cited above, or they may be more concerned with general movements, trends or tendencies, with particular cases as examples of, or exceptions to, such movements. The concern of this book is also with such general movements or trends and I shall make no attempt to compare various accounts of specific events in order to produce a true picture of what happened. Apart from the often very great difficulty of such an attempt (particularly in cases where many participants have since changed sides) there is a danger of getting bogged down in specific details and of ignoring more general, and in the long run more significant, features. Such a concentration on 'the facts', all too common in political journalism and much of political science, tends not only to ignore but also to obscure the less immediately transparent social and economic structures.*

It is, nevertheless, possible to discover a number of common features in the various myths and these, together with the tentative conclusions reached above, serve to establish land-marks, points of reference, for the subsequent discussion of change. Such points of agreement apart, however, each type of myth or collection of stories could provide the basis of an account of the changing pattern of party activity and each such account would no doubt contain some element of truth. Yet none of these would be entirely satisfactory. Any adequate account would have to provide also an account of social and geographical distribution of these myths. Thus, while the myths provide some evidence relating to the past, they must also be treated as features of the present situation which need to be explained. It is in this respect that the examination of myths in terms of the world views, political attitudes and assumptions which they reveal in those who propagate or accept them,

---

* cf. Hoggart's comment: 'You do not learn more about Mr Shepilof by knowing that he draws doodles of horses at the conference table; you only escape the real problems. As the "personalisation" technique becomes yearly more machine tooled, so a good instinct is pulled out of shape and used for oversimplifications, soft deceptions and perilous distortions'. R. Hoggart, *The Uses of Literacy*, London, 1957, p. 169.

or in terms of the functions they serve for such people, is particularly important. In the absence of reliable data – and often in the absence even of unreliable data – any attempt at such an analysis leaves itself open to serious objection. Nevertheless the refusal to examine prevailing accounts of politics in such terms would represent at best an evasion of responsibility by a sociologist or political scientist.

On the right wing of the Labour Party are myths which make a sharp distinction between normal and disturbed situations, between stalwarts and trouble-makers.[4] Normally, in solid Labour areas, the Labour Party hardly exists except at election times. Between elections the party organization tends to wither away, for members are able to rely on their elected leaders to look after them and there is little for the party organization to do. Military analogies are common: 'It's extremely difficult to keep the soldiers at their peak of efficiency when there isn't any war.' The rank-and-file are troops, political fodder, whom the leaders understand better than the trouble-makers who claim to speak for them.

Nevertheless, even in normal situations the party does not wither away entirely. There are still many stalwarts, people who are in general agreement with the party and are also concerned with achieving something in the local community, with a sort of social work. Here special cases of hardship can be brought up in the M.P.'s or councillors' surgery particularly in cases where normal, official channels have proved ineffective. The members who carry out such work find plenty of practical, down-to-earth reasons for fighting to keep the party going – even if they don't understand some of the more esoteric details of party policy.

This happy combination of political inactivity and good works was on occasion rudely disturbed – more so, it seems, during the late 1940s and 1950s than of late. In such cases a few individuals infiltrate the party, bring their supporters in and arrange for them to be elected to the management committee. This minority, acting from political motives and supported by members with personal grudges, are able to influence many of the otherwise solid members and persuade them to attack the leadership, local MP.s or councillors. Sometimes the situation gets so bad that the regional office, or the N.E.C., has to step in and investigate, and some such troublemakers may be expelled. However, they or their allies are often able to control union branches and may be delegated from them to party committees. They are very difficult to get rid of. A few such trouble-makers even get elected to the council and their activity often gives the local party a bad name.

Such myths, which may be more or less paranoic in their fear of communist or Trotskyist subversion, are not particularly common at the grass-roots level. Nevertheless they still have their supporters among local leaderships and, less frequently, among M.P.s – particularly among the older local leaders or M.P.s, who have come up the hard way from working-class origins. Many such leaders have been members of the Communist Party or of various sectarian organizations in the past. Industrial versions of the basic myth have more widespread support within the party, not least from many of the union officials who are also politically active.

More widespread, particularly in the middle-class areas and among party officials, is a myth which, in many respects, is a sober, more dispassionate version of the above. Once again political inactivity is the norm in solid Labour areas but this is no longer simply, or often at all, because there is little need for party work. As far as this is concerned party organization is perhaps less important generally than it is in Conservative or marginal areas – for it is only in these latter areas that the general background of sympathy for Labour, Socialism, the compassionate society or what have you, is lacking.

Nevertheless, on this type of view, the party organization is too weak in many working-class areas for, particularly in

recent years, turnout is occasionally so low that the Conservatives win. Furthermore, many apparently safe Labour
areas depend on an influx of canvassers from the middle-
class areas to get the vote out – often these will be the family
or friends of the candidate from his home party. The reasons given for this sad state of affairs are many and various.
Perhaps the simplest explanation is in terms of various
features of the organization of party meetings. There is too
much time devoted to minutes, correspondence, reports of
officers, reports of councillors, reports of delegates to other
bodies, and all the usual chores. 'In our ward, of course,
we keep that sort of stuff to a minimum.' There is little
in all this to attract or stimulate new members. In many
cases they can go for months 'without hearing anything
authoritative about the party's problems and actions; for
years without ever discussing "socialism"'.[5]

In such an atmosphere members may be attracted by the
noisiness and articulateness of some of the more extreme
elements and, perhaps, become permanently 'opposition-
minded'. To some extent, it is thought, this may be
alleviated by separating the organization of party administration and electioneering from the discussion of policy,
from theoretical argument. In this way neither political
discussion nor the electoral machine need suffer. In view
of the earlier discussion of political interests it is clear that
such a proposal is most likely to prove acceptable to
members in the more middle-class areas.

While it is widely accepted that some such reorganization
can make some difference (officials are generally sceptical
about the chances of this being achieved) it is generally
recognized that this organizational explanation is insuffi-
cient. Many, for example, notice that the working-class
areas are poorly represented in other voluntary associations
of which they are members; others recognize that all
political parties have organizational problems in the more
working-class areas. Thus it is often said that the working
class are not joiners. Or, more specifically, 'lets face it,

politics is a middle-class occupation.' Such a view, of course, assigns honorary membership of the middle classes to many of the working class who live in the right sort of area.

Here explanations relate both to the nature of politics and to the nature of working-class life and are often remarkably similar to Michels' explanation of the apathy of the masses. On the one hand there is the complexity of politics, the need for broad perspectives, for taking the long view, for expert advice and so on. On the other hand the general conditions of working-class life, their educational disadvantages, independent television and so on, make it particularly difficult for them to achieve such long views or broad perspectives, to detach themselves from their immediate situation. Many of them are too tired at the end of the day to even think of political activity. None of this, of course, is said to be their fault. On the contrary, the Labour Party exists to do something about this situation but (for we must be realistic) this is the situation we have to work with.

Involved in such accounts of the present is the recognition, often more implicit than explicit, that the situation in the past was not like this. Sometimes it is said that the early post-war years were an exceptional period and that the party has since reverted to its pre-war norm in the working-class areas under the influence of increasing prosperity, television and commercial bingo. More widespread, however, are vague references to heroic periods in the past when the party organization was first built up or rebuilt after the war. The Welfare State (for all its faults), increasing prosperity, television, have produced a situation which no longer calls forth such heroism (though there is still a lot to be done). The earlier grass-roots activists did a good job, of course, but many of the old problems have been solved and the old sort of activist is, frankly, a bit out of place these days.

Furthermore, it is often argued, the 1944 Education Act made a lot of difference. The people who would have been party activists in those areas in the old days, nowadays have gone to grammar school or even university and have settled in the better-off areas. Quite a few of them were, of course, held back by the education system but even so the natural leaders, the bright and energetic, don't stay in those areas any longer than they have to. The only good party workers in the working-class areas are thought to be those left over from the old days (and many of them are past it really) or a few younger activists who won't stay there very long. In such a fashion many of the middle-class activists, particularly those with working-class backgrounds, seem able to convince themselves that they would have been the natural political leaders or spokesmen of the working-class areas.

The danger from Trotskyists or Communists is, on this sort of view, often exaggerated. Of course they were quite active at one time and there are still a few of them around today. Their arguments are often superficially attractive, particularly to the inexperienced members, but most people get over their sort of approach pretty quickly. Anyway, they perform several quite useful functions really and are often better at first involving people in politics. Many solidly respectable activists will admit that they were that way inclined at one time.

Such views shade over to the Right, as in the type discussed above, or to at least one variety of the self-consciously Left. In the latter case, apart from the reasons listed above, the organizational weakness of the party is attributed to policy. A more full-blooded socialist approach, it is thought, would soon revive the flagging morale of the working-class supporters. Nationalization is sometimes mentioned in this context but far more common are progressive taxation, more spending on schools, hospitals, and so on. Very occasionally the topic of industrial democracy, workers' control, crops up. This, however, is seen as primarily a policy issue, something for the Labour Party to promise, for a Labour government to institute. It has to be achieved through the proper channels. This is the essence, for this group, of democratic socialism and many at least believe that it can be achieved if only the party will stop playing for safety.* As a call to action it is directed primarily towards the party or its leadership. Phrases such as 'The Labour Government must . . .' or 'Harold Wilson ought to . . .' are common. It is not a call for the working class to do anything.

For those who hold such views the past of the Labour Party is littered with debris of many battles between 'the Left' and 'the Right': at conferences, in the constituencies, in the unions. At times it seems almost as if these are seen as two disembodied forces struggling for the soul of Labour. At other times 'the Left' seems to be embodied, on the one hand, in the constituencies and, on the other, in Bevan and others of the Left Labour pantheon. The present situation in the party is seen as the result of earlier Left defeats – because 'the Right' controlled the unions or the party machinery, because of Bevan's final betrayal. Again there are more or less paranoiac versions of the basic myth. In the city party at least such views, like the central dispassionate myths, are found in the middle-class or lower middle-/skilled working-class areas though they come as often from working-class as from middle-class members.

Finally, among the relatively coherent accounts of the present state of the party, is another variety of the self-consciously Left. Here there is little liking for the party and little importance is attached to constitutional niceties. For such members the Labour Party is important not for its policy or its organization but, like it or not, this is where the working class are to be found. 'The political institutions of the Labour Movement have resulted from long and hard struggles of workers for their emancipation. They will not easily die, however much they are abused and turned

* In many respects *Tribune* can be seen as a spokesman for the group. R. Miliband, *Parliamentary Socialism*, London, 1961, gives perhaps the most complete version of this basic left myth.

against their original purposes. Moreover in many parts of the country, and particularly in the north, the Working Man's Club, the Miners' Welfare or the Labour Union rooms remain the centre of political and cultural life of the great mass of workers.'*

On this view membership carries with it no particular identification with the present-day Labour Party. Any such identification is purely residual. The party is simply an arena within which serious political work has to be done: to remain outside the party would be to miss great opportunities for socialist development. The weakness of the political institutions of the Labour Movement is accounted for in terms of their abuse and distortion at the hands of their leaders. The Labour Party has taken on many of the functions of the capitalist state and this is realised, even if they cannot express it in so many words, by more and more of its working-class supporters. Nevertheless these supporters have yet totally to reject the party. For these members, also, the past is littered with defeats.

Such views do not have widespread support within the party. They belong, rather, to individuals here and there: professionals, mostly younger and particularly academics or teachers, and shop stewards. Few remain for long within the party, at least not while retaining such views. In exceptional cases however, where both types of member get together, they may be able to dominate one or more ward parties. Their chances of expulsion are very high. Such groups are rarely found in the two most working-class types of area.†

In the more working-class areas themselves there are few such well formulated myths although rather despairing versions of the basic central and respectable Left myths may sometimes be found. These apart, however, there are many fragmentary, and often contradictory, stories: of Left-wing trouble-makers, of betrayal of this or that councillor, of

* Quoted from M. Barratt Brown, 'The May Day Conference – A Personal View', *May Day Manifesto Bulletin*, no. 5, May 1968, p. 17.
† See also 'A Note on Sects and Factions', in Chapter Six.

corruption, of interference in ward decisions, of the fact that 'they' do not really care about our problems, or that many people make unrealistic demands because they do not really understand the job of a councillor.

There are some stories of the odd 'good' councillors or party leaders but these appear to reflect a particularly ambivalent attitude. On the one hand there are those who are 'good' because they talk the same language as the members, represent the expressed concerns of the ward members and generally fight for 'us' against 'them' – sometimes even going so far as to lead a strike, organize the occasional spectacular fight against eviction, and so on. Such councillors are rarely popular with their colleagues or with corporation officials. Thus, while they certainly appear to represent the interests and concerns of much of the membership, they are not very good at getting things done. Few councillors remain in this position very long and there are therefore many stories of betrayal by such apparently 'good' councillors.

On the other hand are the councillors who are more clearly representative of 'them' than of 'us'. Such councillors talk the language of their colleagues and of corporation officials and are often, if they make the effort, quite effective in getting things done. Thus the category of 'good' councillors includes many of the hard-working adherents to the political orientation common in the solidly non-Labour areas. These, while dealing effectively and energetically with many particular cases, deny the political significance attached to these cases by the members who bring them up. In such areas, then, there exists the paradoxical situation that those councillors who accept the legitimacy of the political orientation of many activists in these areas are generally ineffective while those who deny this legitimacy are generally the most effective. Both types of 'good' councillor, particularly the latter, are frequently hurt by the aggression and lack of gratitude which they experience.

Most members in these areas, including the old stalwarts as well as those with the above ambivalent and contradictory attitudes, offer a wide variety of explanations for the changing number of activists: television, bingo, Bevan or Gaitskell, the changing population of the area, and so on. Here, also, there is the occasional reference to the battles of the past, but these are rarely seen as part of a process of change leading up to the present. Rather they are seen as belonging to a period, long since past, in which that sort of thing used to happen. The absence of such battles reflects the change from the old days to the present normal situation.

Common to the above myths, and to many of the stories, is the recognition, which is at least implicit, that the state of the party organization was different in the past. The suggestion, for example, that the party organization tends to wither away in safe Labour areas implies an earlier period in which the party was built up, the area made safe for Labour, before the setting in of normal politics. Most versions of the past agree that party organization was larger and stronger, or at least that members were more active, in the working-class areas for at least some of the time between now and the end of the war.

Similarly it is agreed that the party has a larger active membership in the middle-class areas than it once had. For some, this is seen as part of the general distortion of the political institutions of the Labour Movement, or as resulting from a deliberate attempt by the leadership to woo the middle classes at the expense of working-class support. For others it is a natural consequence of the growing complexity of politics, increasing prosperity and the growth of the Welfare State, and particularly of compulsory education and the post-war growth of education at the secondary and higher levels.

Thus the broad changes suggested by the preliminary estimate reported above are generally accepted by adherents of most versions of the past. It is not possible, however, on the basis of such agreed features to say very much either about the extent or the timing of changes in party membership. Nor, of course, is there much agreement on the causes or significance of these changes.

As far as the extent of change is concerned proponents of the various Left-wing myths and of some versions of the Right-wing myth tend, though for very different reasons, to give the largest estimates. Others, and particularly many full-time party officials, take what they believe to be a more sanguine, more realistic, view and feel that, although there has been some change, it should not be exaggerated.

Differences over the timing of change reflect, to some extent, disagreement over the place of the various local and national party battles in the process of change. Of course many of the national battles associated, say, with the Bevanite disputes or the later battles over disarmament or Clause Four were reflected in a number of local disputes. Apart from such reflections of national fights, other battles within local parties or between a ward party and its parent constituency or city body have also been fought over the adoption of candidates, attempts to control sitting councillors or M.P.s, rent control and other housing disputes, and so on. Such disputes have occurred at different times in different places and in many areas where party activity has declined no such disputes appear to have taken place.

While this does not mean that such battles have no connexion with changes in membership, it is clear that such changes cannot be explained simply by reference to these battles. It will be argued later that local battles, particularly those in which the national or regional party organization interferes, have played an important part in the more general long-term process of change. Here it is necessary to recognize that the consequences of local disputes are not confined to the immediate battleground.

It is generally only in the case of the various Left myths that such battles are seen as part of the process of change in the membership structure of the party. In other cases, the significance of such battles is seen as relating to the policy or public image of the party. As far as membership is concerned, changes are thought not to be particularly large and have occurred gradually over a period of time. Thus, in the working-class areas, there has been a withering-away of the party organization which is explained either in terms of the military analogy, the difficulty of keeping the troops at the peak of efficiency when there is no war, or in terms of a slow process of attrition brought about by the ageing of the earlier activists and the effects of prosperity, education and rehousing on the rest.

In all but the Left myths, the decline in the working-class areas is not seen as being in any way to do with differences of political interest between members in different types of area. The only exceptions relate either to the sloughing-off of the Trotskyists, Communists and fellow-travellers (all politically motivated men) or to the restricted social horizons of many in the working-class areas.

The Right Labour myth, particularly in its more para-noiac versions, is such that those who accept it are unable to recognize that party members (Trotskyists apart) can have political interests which differ from their own – or, perhaps more generally, which are not compatible with their own. On the contrary, precisely because strictly political activity is no longer necessary (apart, of course, from that of the stalwarts who use the party as a sort of social work agency), anyone who tries to stir up political activity must be a trouble-maker however much he or she may claim to repre-sent the local membership or the working-class.

Many older local leaders and a number of Labour M.P.s seem to have acquired such an orientation during earlier stages of their political careers. Such orientations no doubt allowed for a very effective style of political action during the internal Labour Party strife of the late 1940s and 1950s. However effective they may have been in the past, they are hardly conducive to what, in the middle-class areas, passes for political discussion. If anything, such orientations lead to a style of argument which offends the sensibilities of activists in these areas.

With the increasing domination of the party by the middle-class areas, this type of myth appears to be dying out and has been superseded by the second major type of myth discussed above. However, those who accept this myth are also unable to recognize the real differences in political interests between members in different areas. They may, of course, admit that there appears to be such a conflict but, with their greater detachment and familiarity with the political facts of life, they can see that these appearances are deceptive. Many of the concerns of the more working-class areas are seen as being not really political – though it may be necessary to treat them as such around election time.

Such a myth purveys, and provides effective support for, the definitions of, and orientations to, politics current in the middle-class areas. Many local battles are thus seen as not being really political, as perhaps being stirred up by outsiders but more likely being led by politically inexperienced youngsters or by councillors who really should know better. In any case, the result is that people get worked up about something they don't understand or they get involved in forms of action which are simply counterproductive – rent strikes, resisting bailiffs, and so on. Of course, the party has to put a stop to this sort of thing but it's in their own interests in the long run. Party discipline, then, is exercised more in sorrow than in anger.

Supporters of the Left myths, on the other hand, attribute the decline in working-class areas to political factors and political differences – rather than, say, to the indirect effect of non-political factors on politics. Those who accept the first type are, however, primarily concerned with the general policy level and, in this respect, their position is very similar to that which dominates the party in the middle-class areas. Local battles are seen as manifestations of the national 'Left–Right' battle. Thus, the 'Left' position is attributed to the party activists in the working-class areas – or, if not to the actual activists, at least to the vast numbers of potential activists who would be attracted back by the right policy.

Once again, then, proponents of this type of myth know the real interests of the working-class areas better perhaps than the members themselves. Once again many of the concerns voiced by members in these areas are seen as not really political. Conversely, to many activists in these areas, such Left-wingers are simply a sub-group of 'them'.

Finally, supporters of the other variety of Left myth are often more sympathetic to the expressed concerns of activists in the working-class areas. Furthermore, they often provide support and background services in industrial disputes, rent strikes and other activities which are frowned upon by more respectable sections of the party. However this group also is rather estranged from the activists in the working-class areas. Partly, no doubt, this is due to their apparently esoteric language but it is also a consequence of the fact that this group is generally no more successful than any other in effectively representing the concerns of party members. If anything, their effectiveness complements that of the orthodox representatives of 'them', and they are used accordingly. Activists in these areas have strongly ambivalent attitudes towards both groups. They both have real, but severely limited, services to offer.

It is now possible to sketch the process of change which had led up to the present state of the grass-roots organization of the Labour Party – this process of course has far wider connections and implications which will be discussed later. No attempt will, however, be made to give precise quantitative expressions to these changes: because the relevant data is not available; and because the quantitative aspect of these changes is not the most important.

In part, the following account is in terms of the interaction of the orientations outlined above and of the political interests and definitions discussed in the previous chapter – or rather political action and reaction will be discussed in terms of such orientations, interests and definitions. Such action and reaction will in turn be located within the modified version of Michels' model introduced in Chapter Two.

Conflict and Change

The past state of the Labour Party's grass-roots organization is not at all clear. Nevertheless, it is possible to take, say the rebirth of formal politics at the end of the war as a base point and to describe, in very broad terms, developments since then. The immediate post-war years see attempts, both at the grass-roots level and from the national or regional party organization, to reconstruct or to revitalize the party. Up to the late 40s or early 50s, then the basic picture was one of growth in both active and passive membership. This growth, of course, was very uneven with some local parties growing quickly, others more slowly, and some not at all. In all but the middle-class areas, it will be remembered, a majority of present activists had joined the party during this period. The published membership figures also show a fairly steady growth until the early 1950s. Even though the significance of the precise figures is not clear the recorded growth is impressive.

In at least the early stages of this process, party members, officials and leaders were, whatever their other differences, agreed on the importance of rebuilding the party. Outside the sphere of party organization, an over-riding and generally agreed concern with reconstruction (including housing), tended to obscure other differences. In this period, to use Rex and Moore's expression, the city Labour Party functioned, or was thought to function, as the political instrument of the relatively underprivileged housing classes.[6] In the early stages of this process, housing policy would be judged primarily in terms of urgency, of broad efficiency criteria, by the vast majority of party members, officials or supporters.

However, the post-war growth of council house building, leading to a situation in which the relevant sections of the population had either been rehoused or had members of their family or friends rehoused, led also to the progressive rejection of this particular orientation towards housing by Labour supporters in the more working-class areas – and to a very different type of rejection by Tory supporters elsewhere.

Thus the differentiation, described in earlier chapters, of policy orientation with regard to housing is something which developed gradually and unevenly in different areas during the later 1940s and throughout the 1950s. This development depended, at least in part, on the successes of policies, both national and local, arising out of earlier, more basic concerns with quantity.

With the changing employment situation, the extension of nationalization by public corporation, the decline of rationing and general shortages, a similar differentiation developed in other policy areas – not necessarily at the same time or to the same extent. This differentiation of political interests and of more general policy orientations and implicit definitions of politics would, even without the further developments indicated below, lead to a certain amount of conflict in local parties – particularly in those areas where a small minority of working-class militants were available to form a nucleus for one of the conflicting groups. The significance of such minorities will be discussed briefly below.

At the same time, although the differences of interest between the leaders, both local and national, and the led were never really absent, success in rebuilding the grass-roots organization of the party meant that such differences became increasingly significant. The attitudes of the party leadership towards grass-roots activity thus became increasingly ambivalent. Hence, for example, the setting up of the Wilson Committee on Party Organization whose report appears to have been almost totally ignored.[7]

Cutting across and, to some extent, confusing the above divisions were the complex policy disputes within the national party which tended to polarize along the Left–Right dimension. In such a situation tension between different sections of the party was unavoidable. Often it would break out into open conflict, in other cases this was prevented by means of informal threats or pressure. While some cases of tension or of open conflict may be explained primarily in terms of, say, the Left–Right polarization, it is clear that in general the situation was rather more complex.

It is, of course, the case that such conflicts occurred at different times in different areas and that they often appeared to be very different in kind. In part these differences in, for example, timing are attributable to local differences in the housing or employment situation or in the rate and extent of growth in the grass-roots membership – for the differentiation of policy orentiations was to a large extent dependent on developments in the various policy areas, and so on.

Nevertheless, in spite of many local variations, there are a number of features common to many, if not all, of the local conflicts and disputes of the late 1940s and 1950s. Perhaps the most significant point, at least as far as the grass-roots organization is concerned, relates to differences in basic orientations towards politics in the different areas. It was argued earlier that the dominant orientation in the middle-class areas is towards politics, at both local and national level, as concerned primarily with the provision and maintenance of basic background or environmental services within which individuals can make their own personal decisions – at least as far as their own interests are concerned. Politics is also viewed as being concerned with the provision of services, such as housing, for those who are unable to provide these for themselves. In both cases it is a matter for broad policy discussion and for expert, efficient administration.

In general this orientation is quite compatible with the

growing bureaucratization and centralization of the party machine and of politics as a whole. Thus activists in the middle-class areas are likely to support the claims of local and national leaderships to be the appropriate policy-making bodies. In particular they will condemn local rebellions against policy decisions and, when such rebellions break out, they are the natural allies of the party leadership.

This is not to say, of course, that they will support or agree with the decisions made by the leadership. In the case of disagreement, however, the thing to do is to attempt to change the policy through the proper channels, through discussion, debate, persuasion. Thus they are likely to frown upon many of the tactics used by working-class groups in housing disputes, unofficial strikes and so on.

The history of the Campaign for Nuclear Disarmament illustrates the strength and persistence of such orientations even among the more radical of the middle classes.[8] Hence the persistent refusal of the campaign proper to countenance the use of force, the emphasis on co-operation with the authorities, the reliance on the 'democratic' machinery of the Labour Party, and so on. The recent vogue for participation in planning suggests that this orientation may, at least, be breaking down in some cases. I will return to this point later. For the moment it is sufficient to suggest that continuing developments in the sphere of planning have led to a situation in which political decision impinges more frequently on what, in the middle-class areas, was the proper sphere of personal, private, decision.

However, whether or not this position is now changing, it is clear that, in past disputes between different sections of the local party, combatants from the middle-class areas could often expect support from the regional or national party organization. Similarly in disputes between a particular local party and the national or city leadership – over, for example, the adoption of candidates or the re-adoption of sitting members[9] – the leadership could expect support, if only in principle, from the activists in the middle-class areas. In such cases, as I have already pointed out, the party constitution acts as a very useful and effective weapon in the hands of those who are most familiar with them. Once again, because of the number of interests involved, it is a very rare conflict that represents one or other of the pure types indicated above. When such conflicts start, and often before they break out into the open, there is a tendency for anyone else around, if they have anything to gain or to lose, to pitch in.*

City and national leaders and party officials are particularly concerned with two sorts of objective: the preservation of the organization; and the preservation or improvement of their own position within the organization. There is, of course, an understandable tendency for them to identify these two objectives. Indeed they are supported in this identification by some sections of the membership – particularly from the more middle-class areas of the city. Given this situation, there are a number of more or less constitutional ways of achieving these ends. Where these fail there are other possibilities: the expulsion or non-admittance of members; and, so it is sometimes alleged, the fixing of party elections or meetings.

During the late 1940s and early 1950s and to a lesser extent since then – one can hardly expect a party to keep up a high rate of expulsion – there were a number of occasions when members were expelled from the party. Often this involved the closing down and later reconstitution of ward and constituency parties. As for the 'fixing' of meetings, it would not be difficult for the city or regional organization to find grounds for challenging the credentials of some of those present, or if necessary to, say, provide suitable members with appropriate membership cards. Certainly it is not difficult for an apparently sympathetic outsider to be provided with a number of allegations concerning this sort of thing. Even if, or when, there is

* Local newspapers in particular.

nothing to such allegations it is clear that they are still significant indicators of the state of mind of many party members– and of any number of ex-members.

It is hardly surprising that these allegations are most frequent in the most working-class areas. There are several reasons for this: members in these areas are, as has already been pointed out, very likely to be dissatisfied and therefore likely also, according to one type of counter-allegation, to cause trouble; alternatively such allegations could be seen simply as indications of discontent; at the same time, at least from the point of view of the leadership, the most important decisions left to the lower levels of the organization concern the selection of candidates for local or national elections. Thus it is the wards or constituencies that are relatively safe that are most likely to come into conflict with the party hierarchy.

Such extreme cases, if they occur at all, are hardly everyday events, and indeed it is hardly necessary that they should be. On the one hand informal, more or less constitutional, pressures, appeals to party loyalty and so on, may well be sufficient to bring any dispute to a satisfactory conclusion. Thus one researcher reports the case of a particularly able and successful regional organizer who: 'told the author that the main reason why so few anti-leadership candidates were adopted by the C.L.P.s in his region was that he made it his business to see that they were kept off short lists whenever he could prevent it. Any regional organizer who does not do the same, he felt, is not doing his job properly.'[10]

On the other hand a very few examples may serve to encourage other members to be more realistic in their activities. Here also it should be pointed out that, even when the party hierarchy strictly follows the constitution, this behaviour need not be accepted as either fair or reasonable – whether by those directly involved or by those who hear about it later.

Such developments can lead to the loss of members

either directly through expulsion or resignation or in-directly through a decline in activity and a failure to rejoin at the end of a year. A less obvious consequence is the atrophy, in many areas, of the formal party structure. This follows partly through a loss of activists and partly because informal contacts appear to many members, particularly those who use the party as a sort of social work agency, to be more effective ways of getting some sort of action.

In this latter process the role of those M.P.s and local leaders who accept the type of Right-wing myth outlined above, who have come up the hard way, is particularly important. Their hard-hitting political style, sustained by the conviction that they understood their troops better than anyone else, and involving appeals to loyalty and a near populist stance, was often successful in destroying political opposition within the party. Furthermore the political background of such leaders enabled them to talk the language of the working-class areas; the language of, for example, ruined housing, blocked drains, of plumbing and the shortage of toilets, or of hygiene and public health.

In the earlier post-war years the use of such a language, implying as it does a distrust of the bureaucratic rationality of the housing department and of officials and intellectuals in general, was often effective in maintaining support for the leader, if not for winning over the dissident activists. It will be remembered that, in terms of this myth, such dissaffected troops must be under the influence of outsiders – either Trotskyists and fellow-travellers or intellectuals. The appeal of such leaders was based on a distrust of official machinery (either within the party or in the local authority) and of intellectuals and outsiders. It was a personal rather than an organizational appeal.

Party members were encouraged to take their problems to the charismatic individual rather than to work through the formal machinery of the party or the local authority. Hence the tendency of the party organization in these areas to wither away: the more political activists being defeated and the problem-orientated activists depending on personal contacts. The danger for the party here, of course, is that, particularly after a period of internal conflict, such informal structures may be personally loyal to, and also dependent on the local party leader.

During the reign of such leaders the withering-away of the party organizations, at least in part, in the working-class areas allowed the wards in the middle-class areas to consolidate their hold over the formal organization of the party – often without opposition. The gradual replacement of these leaders by a new generation from a very different background involves the progressive collapse of many of the remaining informal structures in the working-class areas – the rate of collapse increasing as the earlier leaders age, retire, die, and as their contacts age with them.

These and other processes are of course cumulative in their effect and lead many local parties in the long run into a vicious circle of decline. Thus a ward party with only a few old and often bitter members, with very little coherent discussion but with many long and, to outsiders, hardly coherent reminiscences, with little power and very little contact with other sections of the party, is hardly likely to attract, or to retain, new members. With few new members, and even fewer who remain, the ward party is likely to decline further and faster and become even less worth joining.

It is hardly necessary to emphasize that such processes are unlikely to affect the more middle-class areas where the political views, if any, of Labour candidates are of little concern to the city or national party. In these areas, in fact, the situation is one of slow, and sometimes rapid, growth of membership. Here again the effect is cumulative. More and more councillors will tend to come from these wards and will discuss local policy and changes therein with the activists there. So the activists in middle-class areas will have some idea of, and perhaps some influence on, how policy decisions come about. Thus some groups of activists, with some justification, see the local party as a fairly democratic organization with many opportunities for the rank-and-file to participate. Activists in other areas see the party rather differently but their relative lack of participation provides further support for the basic central myth described above. In this sense also, a vicious circle appears to be operating which affects the determination of local policy. This in turn pushes the circle a little further round.

Thus, as against both Michels' thesis and Lipset's redefinition,* the party at the city level is experienced as both democratic and undemocratic: there appears for some members to be a basic conflict of interest between the leaders and the rank-and-file while for other groups of members there is no such conflict. The apparent conflict of interest between leaders and members is also a conflict between different sections of the membership. With regard to the national leadership, of course, the situation is rather more complex but the local situation also affects the members' perception of these leaders – particularly when the national party has been instrumental in squashing local rebellions. At the same time the working-class areas of the city do at least return Labour M.P.s and are thus well supplied with opportunities for conflict with the national organization which party members in the middle-class areas so often lack.

The significance of the above changes does not reside simply, or even mainly, in the absolute numbers involved. Among other things these changes affect the position of less active party members and the electorate in general in different areas. The long-term decline in active membership, as in the activity of such members, may affect voting support through the decline in the number of locally known activists who would otherwise function at election time as vote collectors. Thus the local party which is relatively strong in terms of its active support is the better able to

* See Chapter Two.

survive electorally the reactions to Labour government policy. The implication here is, of course, that the present unpopularity of the Labour Party at a national and, to varying degrees, a local level is not simply to be explained as a reaction to government policy. It depends also to a large extent on the long term decline of active Labour support among many sections of the working class: in, for example, the withering away of the formal party organization in the working-class areas of cities and its replacement by informal structures and on the later collapse even of these.

A further consequence of this decline in active support in some areas has been that the determination of local policy is now very largely in the hands of the middle classes, or, more correctly, the middle-class areas. This change should not, of course, be exaggerated, for the Labour Party has never been simply a working-class organization, but the changes in the relative strengths of working-class and middle-class areas is nevertheless significant.

It has led, for example, to a change, both in emphasis and in detail, in the policies adopted at local levels. This in turn affects both the number of local activists and the support for the party at both local and national elections. It should not be surprising if many people in the more working-class areas see little difference between the local policies of the two major parties and have little reason therefore to support either. For all their intolerance of opposition the old style of local leader did at least express themselves in the political language of the working-class areas. To an increasing extent this is now denied them.

This is not to deny that there are differences between the major parties at a local level or that the people who formulate these policies consider the differences important. The point is rather that for many people, given the conditions under which they live and the political demands based on these conditions, the differences are irrelevant. This apathy is reinforced by culturally dominant definitions of politics which increasingly define their concerns as non-political.

This situation leads to the appearance of a near-consensus at the city level for the discontented are no longer even as politically powerful as they once were. Political debate is thus able to centre more round questions of means and less round those of ends.

The significance of such developments at a national level has been obscured to some extent both by the relative infrequency of elections and by the fact that Labour was out of power for so long before the 1964 election. While the weakness of the party organization in many working-class areas did not prevent the victory, it can nevertheless be argued that this weakness was an important factor in the later collapse of electoral support for Labour. The attrition of the lower levels of the formal and informal mechanisms of communication between party leaders and much of their electoral support resulted in a situation where M.P.s' assessment of the feeling in the party bore little relation to the feelings of many who had regularly voted Labour. Since such an assessment is one of the many elements taken into account in policy-making it is possible that, had the grass-roots situation been different, the government would have found it expedient to follow a rather different course of action or at least to sugar the pill. Thus, it may be suggested, the long-term decline in active membership in the working-class areas not only weakens the ability of local parties to ride out the effects of unpopular government actions, but it is one of the factors which made these particular actions possible.

In any event it is clear the changes indicated above are not simply of local significance. Widespread changes at the grass-roots level can affect the higher levels of the party in a large number of ways: through, for example, changes in the personnel involved in selection procedures, in the social and political background of those selected as candidates, in the sort of activists who mix with the local M.P., local leaders and visting party dignitaries.

Taken together such changes represent a change in the

whole character of the party at a city and at a national level. These higher level changes in turn affect the conditions within which local parties operate. Thus, for example, the long-term decline in active membership in the working-class areas does not depend on all of the above processes operating on each ward or constituency party. Ward or constituency parties may well remain strong and avoid involvement in overt conflict or even, in rare cases, win such battles as they are involved in, long after otherwise similar parties have declined. They survive however within a city or a national party which increasingly has no place for them. In such a situation their decline has not been prevented: it is merely delayed.

This sort of mutual interaction between the grass-roots and the higher levels of the party further complicates the problem of analyzing political change. Much of the above analysis has ignored these further complications. The concern has been to examine some of the processes involved in producing the present political situation rather than to produce an accurate historical account. Such an account would have to bring these together with many other processes and events.

Nevertheless, while the above does not pretend to be history (and should not be treated as such), it does, I believe, serve to reveal significant characteristics of contemporary British politics and society. Before considering these characteristics directly there are a number of gaps in the above analysis which must be filled or at least plastered over. This will be the task of the following chapter.

6 Sects, Factions and Other Areas

It is clear from the analysis so far that developments within the city party cannot reasonably be separated from social, political or economic developments within the wider society. Thus it has been argued above that the particular differentiation of political concerns which has occurred within the city party depended in part on developments in the field of housing, employment, and so on. Furthermore the progress of the conflicts of interest arising out of this differentiation of concerns depended, again only in part, on the position of higher levels of the party organization with respect to such conflicts. Conversely it was argued that these other developments in turn depended on what had happened within the city party.

An examination of the significance of the processes discussed above must therefore concern itself with the relationships between these processes and other features of contemporary British society. In particular it is necessary to say something about local Labour Parties outside the cities and to locate the local processes within the context of wider political and economic change. It is not entirely possible to separate these topics, but the emphasis in this chapter will be on the former.

The mutual interaction discussed above between the grass-roots and higher levels of the party suggests one of the ways in which developments in the city parties may affect other areas. Through their influence on higher levels of the party organization, changes in the cities affect the political context in which other local parties operate. However while different types of local party are related by means of the formal machinery of the party they may also be related by other groups which cut across ward and constituency boundaries. Some of these groups will be discussed briefly below, after which the position of non-city local parties will be considered.

A Note on Sects and Factions

This is not the place for a full discussion of the relationships between the various Left groupings, the Communist Party and the Labour Party. Indeed, in the absence of any systematic study of such relationships, and given the place such groups occupy within the mythology propagated by many political and industrial leaders, no adequate discussion is possible at present. It is nevertheless both possible and necessary to make a few points here.[1]

Of course, not all cross-cutting groups are to the Left of the Labour Party. Ideally all such groups should be discussed but, as far as the politics of the working class are concerned, it is the various Left-wing sects or factions which are particularly significant. Many of these latter groups achieve only a momentary, localized existence; others, however, attain a relatively permanent national organization. It is primarily with this type of group, operating just within or just without the party organization, that the following will be concerned.

In the discussion of political myths current within the Labour Party, two broad types of self-consciously Left positions were distinguished. For one of these the Labour Party, together with other political institutions of the Labour Movement, has been abused and turned against its original purposes. Members in this position have no particular liking for the party but believe that it is necessary for socialists to work within the Labour Party because this is where the politically conscious members of the working class are to be found.

The position of such members is politically uncomfortable for several reasons. On the one hand they engage in forms of political action which are unlikely to endear them to the local or national party leadership. In fact their justification for joining the party is precisely the opportunity it provides for much action. They are thus in constant danger of expulsion and must maintain a balance between the desirability of action and the danger this action would bring.

On the other hand such members are well aware of those who have moved from this position, either into a more respectable Left position (and often much further Right), or out of the party into one or other of the sects, the Communist Party, or political inaction. Furthermore, partly because of the tensions involved in their own position, they are continually tempted to move one way or the other themselves.

This position then serves as an ideological transition zone or border post with orthodox politics to one side and unorthodox politics to the other – with traffic and communications going in both directions. At no time are the numbers involved in this position particularly high – and most of these will be in transit.

Nevertheless, groups of such activists do sometimes achieve a local significance and, in these cases, their actions and the party's reactions will often be communicated to similar groups elsewhere through the medium of the nationally organized groups or factions.

Some such groups operate primarily as discussion groups with occasional canvassing forays into the outer world. The members then provide mutual support for both their opposition to the party leadership and their active support of this leadership at election times. Such groups provide little or no threat to the local leadership and their members are particularly likely to move into politically more respectable positions.

More of a threat is posed by the other, more active, types

of group. Apart from organizing continual pressure within the party on local M.P.s or councillors, they may also be involved in other types of local initiative: helping to organize or provide tactical support for local unofficial strikes, rent strikes and other means of putting pressure on local officials, preventing evictions, and so on. Members of such groups are, as I have already argued, often sympathetic to the concerns expressed in the more working-class areas: particularly so in the case of many of those concerns which party leaders and councillors see as unrealistic.

These members, then, are particularly likely to become involved in local political battles: not so much as causes of such battles but more as advisors to, and tacticians for, one side. The results of such battles are communicated to similar groups elsewhere and can thereby affect a far wider range of activists than are directly involved. Thus a relatively small number of scattered local battles can affect the way the party is viewed by a substantial minority of activists throughout the country.

In this way also, then, events in the city parties can affect local parties in other types of area. The extent of these effects depends in part on the numbers involved in this ideological transition zone and, in particular, on the attractiveness of the 'entrist' argument for joining or remaining within the party. To the extent that this entrist position has support, the experience of local opposition groups within the party can be transmitted to other such groups. However, the more effective such groups are in this respect, the more they come to the attention of local and national party leaders and the more useful they become for the purposes of political scapegoating.

The entrist position is thus, in a sense, self-destructive, for unless those who support it can muster massive support within the party, their numbers are likely to decline as a result either of expulsion or of voluntary movement to the Right or Left. In part, the decline in the rate of expulsion since the early 1950s is attributable to the decline in this section of the membership. A further consequence of this decline is that local opposition groups within the party become increasingly isolated from other such groups, although some contact may be maintained through official or unofficial union organizations.

However, the decline of the entrist section of the membership has a far wider significance and is by no means an unambiguous answer to the leadership's prayer. In particular, the decline of this section involves a decline in the number of members in transit in both directions. A number of local party leaders and councillors and not a few M.P.s have, in the past, graduated from socialist sects to the Labour Party through this section of the membership. Their political background, then, has involved a political training which more orthodox entrants have never, or very rarely, received. In particular they have entered the party with a familiarity with the language and political concerns of the more working-class areas. Such councillors, local leaders and M.P.s, although always in a minority, can play an important part in maintaining support for the party within some sections of the working class.

With the decline of the entrist sections this mode of entry into formal politics has become less important and these councillors or local leaders are unlikely to be replaced with similar figures. On the contrary they are increasingly likely to be replaced by those who have come into political activity through the Labour Party in the more middle-class areas: by activists who speak the political language of these, rather than of the working-class areas.

More generally, and perhaps in the long run more significantly, this decline signifies, and in part enforces, the increasing divorce of the revolutinary socialist from the social reform tradition in British politics. Thus the, at one time relatively easy, transition from revolutionary socialist outside the party to (rather less) revolutionary socialist within the party to social reformer, and perhaps further across the political spectrum, is becoming increasingly less effective as the great transformer of socialists that it once was.

In many respects this situation has arisen out of the processes, or at least some of them, which have led to the decline of the party in the working-class areas of cities. The position however is very different in the two cases. While the majority of disaffected party members in the working-class areas remain as bitter, carping, ineffective activists, use the party as a sort of social work agency or drop out of politics, the majority of the ideologically committed activists who move out of the party reorganize, or attempt to do so, elsewhere, or, if they are suitably employed, concentrate on industrial activity. Indeed many, who are now politically active (in the broadest sense) on the Left, have never been active within the Labour Party at all but have been recruited directly into what the more orthodox call extremist politics.

This is particularly noticeable, of course, in the case of students who are recruited far less frequently than they would once have been into the Left-wing of the Labour Party – in part because there is less of a Left-wing for them to be recruited into, in part because other Left groupings are less content to be parasitic on Labour. Hence the development of predominately middle-class (professional and student) extreme Left groupings. While many such students may be concerned at their lack of contact with the working class, which would once have been achieved through the Labour Party, they are nevertheless freed from many of the chores and much of the tedium which activity in the party would have brought and, among other things, are able to devote themselves to subjects of more obvious concern to other students.

While it would be a gross oversimplication to explain the growth of revolutionary student movements in such terms, it could nevertheless be argued that the developments described above have played a part in producing the political climate in which such movements have arisen. The initial rejection of the Labour Party, even of its Left-wing, by these movements has meant that the ready-made means of contact with the working class, which would once have been provided by party activity, are no longer available.

The lack of such contact in the early stages of the student movements, and to a large extent even now, may indicate simply that such means of contact must be created afresh, outside the field of political orthodoxy. There are signs that this is being attempted – in small squatters' organizations and in the tenants' or community associations which often deal with issues that would once have been aired through the ward organization of the Labour Party – and that these attempts are sometimes successful, if only for relatively short periods.

It is in irony of contemporary politics that the growth of political action outside the formal political structures is, in part, a consequence of the great success the Labour Party has had in controlling its dissident elements and in incorporating many of the individuals involved; that the party's control over its members or supporters depends in the long run on these members' control over their party. This is the fatal weakness of Social Democracy but the qualification, 'in the long run', is crucial. To the extent that politics is normally defined by the conflict of Labour (or Social Democrat) and other anti-socialist, middle-class parties', disaffection from Labour, for many of the working class (and a still small minority of the middle classes), appears as disaffection from politics, as political apathy. Alternatives, which often appear also to be non-political or, to others, politically illegitimate, are not developed overnight. I shall return to this argument later.

Outside the City

The Labour Party is not likely to be politically important in the most rural areas or in those largely middle-class areas that are locally self-governing. Other urban or partly urban areas may differ from the large city in a number of respects. In view of the earlier discussion of the city as a political unit two of these would appear to be particularly important: there will be neither such a range of living conditions nor such a large degree of residential segregation between the classes. Differences between the living conditions of particular individual families may, of course, be as great as any in the city but the above statement refers to identifiable areas rather than to individuals. The above differences, then, are largely a consequence of differences in population size for, in the smaller urban areas, there are simply not enough people for a wide range of types of area to arise.

Some locally self-governing communities, such as, for example, many mining communities, are very largely working class. In this type of area in particular the politically significant division between middle- and working-class areas hardly arises and, although there may be conflicts between the local and the national party, this need not lead to a decline in support for the local party. In fact it is precisely this type of area that has achieved both a very high turnout at election time and a large Labour majority.

This has usually been taken as evidence for the effects of social pressures on voting behaviour.* Thus it is argued that, since everyone else in the area is a Labour supporter, the political pressures on any particular individual all act in the same direction and there are few confusing cross-pressures to prevent people from making up their minds. So they all vote Labour. Unfortunately for this type of argument, apart from all the problems discussed in Chapter One, there is usually a very low turnout in the city-centre constituencies which have a similarly high proportion of the working class in the electorate. The argument of the preceding chapters would suggest that one of the major reasons for this difference lies in the nature and policies of

* See Chapter One.

the local parties: in particular in the presence or absence within the local party of the division between types of area.

There are also important differences in the trade union structures in the two types of area. Thus general unions, which are notoriously undemocratic at all levels, are strongest in the large cities, while industrial or craft unions are stronger in the more isolated working-class constituencies. Thus in many, but by no means all, cases even the grass-roots union organization may be out of its members' control in the cities while in the relatively isolated mining or steel communities the local branch may retain a great deal of autonomy. Union support for the Labour Party will therefore involve different things and have different consequences in the two types of area.[2]

Thus, in one area, the local party will be largely a working-class organization closely integrated with the local union structure – perhaps with some of the same elected officials. At the other extreme, the party will be far more under the influence of the middle classes and of working-class members who do not live in predominantly working-class areas. Furthermore, apart possibly from a few ward parties, the city party as a whole will be relatively independent of rank-and-file unionism although it may well have the financial and organizational support of the full-time union hierarchy.

This is not, of course, to argue that the local party will remain strong in the more isolated working-class communities. Indeed it is precisely in these areas that, from the point of view of its supporters, a strong and active party organization is hardly necessary. There are several reasons for this: the absence of strong local political opposition and of significant differences in the life styles of members or supporters in different sub-areas limit the chances of a city-like situation developing; the local Union or Labour Club, within which the party may be organized, provides an informal organizational means for putting pressure on, or getting at, local party leaders or local councillors. The party, of course, may still be locally oligarchic but in this case the local leaders would be in no position to develop life-styles totally divorced from those of many of their supporters. In such cases the process of decline, if any, will be different, and will have different consequences, from that in the large cities. Some of these differences will be discussed shortly.

In urban areas which are neither large cities nor predominantly middle or working class the situation will again differ from that in the large city. In these cases, however, the difference will often be one of degree rather than kind, depending on the size of the local government area, the degree of residential segregation between classes, the range of living, and particularly housing conditions and the extent to which the area contains, or is contained in, more or less safe Labour seats. In many such areas the differentiation of political orentiations towards housing, and all that goes with it, may not have the opportunity to develop to the same extent as in the cities. Here, even if the party is dominated by the more middle-class areas, the depoliticizing effect of such domination is likely to be less severe.

The situation is, of course, even more complex in areas where local government is shared between urban or rural district councils on the one hand and a county council on the other. It would take far too long to discuss the complexities here but it is possible to identify a few of the significant differences. As far as the formal party organization is concerned the relations between the constituency and the county party are likely to be far looser than the corresponding relations between constituency and city party. Residential segregation between areas and the range of living conditions may again be as great as, or greater than, those in the cities but the distances involved, the relatively poor communications (as compared to the city), and the partial political autonomy of the separate areas are again likely to reduce the political significance of these differences.* The county, or even the constituency, party may then take on the character of a fairly loose federation.

Nevertheless, in those few counties which are politically dominated by Labour (e.g. County Durham and some parts of Wales and Scotland), those features which in other cases reduce the political significance of area differences have a very different effect. In particular the leaders of the county party may acquire an even great autonomy than their city counterparts. Here the life style of the leaders is based not so much on that of the middle class, or indeed any other, areas. It is based rather on the fact of travel; of living, in a sense, in the whole county rather than in this or that part of it. In these cases even the middle-class members may feel left out of things.

Finally, in this comment on types of area, it is worth mentioning the new town situation. The uniqueness of new towns as far as the argument of this book is concerned lies in the high proportion of middle-class families living in public housing. Here the differentiation of housing conditions, and thus of political orientations towards housing, is of a different degree and kind from that found in almost all other areas. A possible development in such cases, given the similarity of housing conditions, is a strong Labour Party with both middle-class and working-class activists working on the same lines which can maintain its support in spite of the unpopularity of the Labour Government.[3] There are however other possibilities.

In a number of the above areas, then, a relatively strong party may survive with substantial working-class support; either because the area is dominated by the working class or because of a lack of local differentiation between middle- and working-class areas. Thus, whatever else may happen here, the tradition of local political activity may still survive

---

* So, in small towns, may the type of social relationship existing between employer and employee. See in particular the discussion of the effects of new industry in Banbury. M. Stacey, *Tradition and Change*, London, 1960.

among the working class. In England at least, however disillusioned or discontented they may be with the national party, the local organization is unlikely to collapse. The constituency parties may content themselves with selecting as candidates those who do not support all aspects of party policy. In the absence of any suitable conflict within the local party the regional or national organization will find it difficult to prevent this.*

However, in Scotland or Wales the situation is rather different. Here, if an individual can no longer support the Labour Party because of the actions of the Labour Government, he can at least support the local nationalist party instead. In England there appears to be no such alternative for, to the discontented Labour supporter, the Conservative or Liberal Parties may seem even worse. Exceptions to this generalization may occur in England in new towns or in the county boroughs built on the edges of many cities. Here, particularly where there is no strong Liberal tradition in the area, it is possible for the Liberal Party to perform the functions of the new town Labour Party considered above: for, if it is the local organization that matters to supporters, it does not matter too much whether it calls itself Labour or not.

In these cases, more particularly in Scotland or Wales, it is important to note that it is not only individuals who may change their support. Local organizations, or parts of these, may do this also; but only where the organization is still functioning in working-class areas. This is more likely outside the large cities. Of course, one cannot expect all such local organizations to change in this way nor, when they do so, will all the local activists so change. In particular the most prominent activists, those who are publicly identified as Labour, may find it more difficult to change than their grass-roots supporters.

---

* Of course there is always conflict in local parties. What is significant in the city situation, and often elsewhere, is that such conflict often has a social and organizational basis; it is not simply a dispute between similarly situated individuals.

However, in those cases where a majority of activists have changed their support, the local authority may remain under the control of substantially the same local organization. In such cases the problem of divided loyalties among the local electorate is minimized and the Nationalist or Liberal Party takes over what appears to be a ready-made organization. This possibility may help to explain those cases where the Nationalist or Liberal Party is almost non-existent one year and yet takes over the local authority in the next.

Thus one would expect the present nationalist organizations to have more active support among the working class in those industrial areas which are outside the large cities.* Of course it is important not to generalize too far here, for in those areas, say, where the mining industry has declined rapidly in recent years, it seems likely that the Labour Party will remain closely associated with the miners' union and be increasingly remote from the majority of the local working class. In such cases, and also in the large cities, the Nationalists will have to provide their own organization. It seems also likely that if, or when, nationalism becomes powerful in the large cities of Scotland or Wales it will have to face problems similar to those faced by the Labour Party at the moment. Thus, while Nationalist Parties may bring many of the working classes back into political activity in the short-run, the long-term effects may be an even greater disillusion.

* A recent study by the Department of Social Studies at Portsmouth College of Technology claims that, 'especially in smaller towns, the S.N.P. vote violates traditional lines of social and political division by combining hitherto politically opposed groups; e.g. skilled workers and industrial managers'. Quoted in the *Observer*, 10 August 1969.

7   The Changing Face of Politics

In Chapter Four, two broad polar types of orientation were identified – with, of course, all sorts of intervening positions. On the one hand politics was seen as being basically a matter of general principles, of broad policy outlines. Thereafter it is a matter of administration, of getting suitably qualified personnel and of setting up the right sort of machinery to execute policy. Within this broad orientation there is, of course, considerable room for dispute particularly over the sorts of policy area that should come within the scope of political decision. Nevertheless such disputes should not obscure the fact of general agreement as to the sort of thing that politics is and ought to be; the fact that this agreed conception of politics is taken for granted, is not open to question. This orientation corresponds to the experiences of local or national government as providing an environment or background within which people are free to make their own decisions.

On the other hand is an orientation to politics which responds to the experience of unavoidable personal involvement, in the consequences of political decision; to the experience of government, and particularly of local government, as an external constraining and coercive organization. Here the details of policy execution are, or ought to be, political matters.

The distinction here is a little overdrawn for it is entirely possible to have different types of orientation with respect to different policy areas. Such a combination of orientations is particularly common in the more working-class areas for it is precisely here that the sharp distinction between the personal and the political breaks down. In the British context, housing is perhaps the most outstanding policy topic to fall within the area of overlap. It is in this sense that housing has been important in grass-roots political development – not simply as a matter of bricks and mortar but as an area in which, for many people, the most intimate connections between the personal and the political were established.*

Even within a particular policy area those with different types of orientation need not come into conflict, and they may at times be able to support the same policy. Thus, in a situation which is widely recognized as one of acute housing shortage, one general policy demand (build more houses) may be supported by all concerned and judged in fairly similar terms (speed, efficiency, cost, etc.).

It was argued above that, with the growth of public housing programmes, of public housing and the relative decline of private rented accommodation, political demands based on these different orientations and experiences have become progressively more differentiated.† Furthermore, this differentiation has developed within the city Labour Parties: that is, it has not been reflected within the formal structure of politics by, say, a corresponding differentiation between the two major parties (with Labour going one way and the Conservatives going the other).

It would be an oversimplification, therefore, to see the changes in the pattern of membership within the city Labour Parties as representing a change of domination

---

* Within industry the situation is in many respects similar with, on the one hand, a sharp distinction between personal and policy matters and on the other, an intimate connexion between the two. This corresponds very roughly to the differences between the work experience of the manager on the one hand and of the worker on the other. It is one of the great achievements of the Labour Party, and of the Trade Union movement, to have kept these differences from erupting into politics in spite of the attempts of many activists.

† 'Conflict and Change' in Chapter Five.

from one type of orientation to another. Rather the rebirth of formal politics at the end of the war saw, within the Labour Party, a large measure of agreement between political demands based on very diverse basic orientations – at least with respect to policy areas which seemed particularly important at the time. Nevertheless it is certainly the case that the first of the above orientations has increasingly come to dominate the party in the city and in many other areas.

It is important here to note that this latter development is not simply a consequence of local conflicts between the more middle-class areas and the rest. Not only did the outcome of these local conflicts often depend on the intervention, formal or informal, of the party's national organization, but the local conflicts themselves formed part of the larger, national process of the bureaucratization and routinization of decision-making within the Labour Party. Thus this bureaucratization and routinization in part progressed by means of these local conflicts.

In the discussion of Michels' argument in Chapter Two, it was pointed out that the party operates within an environment containing, among other things, large complex and generally undemocratic political, industrial or state organizations. To some extent the bureaucratization and routinization of the decision-making process is a response to the pressures of this institutional environment – given, that is, that the party operates strictly in terms of the established rules and procedures of the society concerned. The party, in other words, adapts itself, and the leaders adapt themselves, to the environment and the forms of this adaptation must be expected to change in accordance with changes in the institutional environment itself.

The processes discussed in earlier chapters must, then, be understood as taking place within a changing institutional environment and as representing the adaptation of the party organization to these changes. Of particular interest here would be the increasing centralization of the

British economy; the growth and increasing importance of large commercial, industrial and state organizations; the spread of large international firms; and so on. These developments have a profound effect on the relationships between government and industry and therefore between political and industrial or commercial organizations. On the one hand government agencies must be concerned, not only with industry in general, but also with what particular firms are up to. Many firms, particularly those operating on an international scale, are now of such a size that a decision by any one of them can affect the outcome of government policy.

On the other hand the larger firms are the more likely to be directly affected by government policy. For some the state is important primarily as a source of finance or as a major customer. For others government action is particularly important precisely because, in the industry concerned, there is not, or is no longer, a state of free competition between many independent producers. In an industry dominated by a few large firms, government action or inaction does not simply affect the general economic environment (as it might in a situation of perfect competition), it affects each of the large firms in a direct and obvious fashion. In the case of the motor industry, for example, deflationary government policy does not have the effect of driving the least efficient firm to the wall: rather it affects the sales and profitability of each of the major producers in very similar ways. Thus, for the large firm, the government is not experienced as maintaining a suitable economic environment within which the firm can operate but, precisely because it can have such a direct effect, as something which the firm should attempt to control or, at least, come to some sort of arrangement with.*

* The reader may notice a certain similarity between the position of the large firm and that of most residents of the more working-class areas of our cities. The crucial differences concerns their bargaining position which is very strong in one case and very weak indeed in the other.

Thus it is in the interests of both government and industry, of political and industrial or commercial organizations, that the two sides should get together. This togetherness does not simply affect the leaders of the organizations concerned for they are all served by an array of bureaucrats and specialists. It is in the interests of each organization that at least some of its specialists should be familiar with the workings of other organizations – so that in its own planning each organization can take the planning procedures of other organizations into account. Hence both sides will be concerned to encourage the exchange of specialists between civil service or party organizations on the one hand and industrial, commercial or union organizations on the other. The development of close relationships between government and industry, politics and business, is further encouraged by, and is partly a consequence of, the growth of the Welfare State and of government responsibility for maintaining full employment, providing education and vocational training, and so on.[1]

It would, unfortunately, take far too long to discuss the effects of these developments on the structure of politics in any detail. Nevertheless it is important to recognize that, in general, the pressures on the Labour Party from the institutional environment towards the increasing bureaucratization and centralization of decision-making, the employment of, and dependence on, specialists, and the emphasis on professional administration, have been entirely consistent with the basic orientation of party activists in the middle-class areas.

This is not to claim, of course, that activists in these areas necessarily supported the policies actually adopted. What they did support, rather, were the apparent forms of policy-making (general principles, board policy outlines, together with specialized, professional execution) and the right of the leadership to make this policy. It is precisely because of the broad and general nature of policy, of the fact that it is a matter of principle, that final decision should be reserved for the higher levels of the party – otherwise there is a danger of confusing political and administrative decisions.

Thus the processes of change in the city, and other local, parties discussed above have resulted from an alliance of the party leadership and activists in the middle-class areas against many, but not all, of the rest, and from the overall victory of this alliance. While this victory has left the middle-class areas, or rather the activists therein, with substantial control of their local parties this is not to say that they now control the national party. The situation here is rather complex for, to the extent that the interests of the party leadership and the general orientations of these activists do not conflict, the question of control is not really put to the test.

Even such control as they possess at the local level is severely limited: in internal party matters, to that which is left them by the national party organization; in policy matters, to those remaining areas of local authority decision which are not concerned simply with local administration of national government policy. It is precisely the demands for greater local autonomy that were defeated in the inner-party battles of the post-war years. Indeed the political orientations of these activists have led them in general to support the autonomy of the leadership and the growth of the party bureaucracy.

Furthermore, the alliance between these sections of the rank-and-file and the party leadership depends crucially on the particular orientation towards politics described above. This orientation, based as it is on the rigid distinction between the political and the personal spheres, is in no sense an innate characteristic of those living in the middle-class areas. On the contrary it depends on a particular way of experiencing politics and government; on the experience of local and national government as providing and maintaining an environment in which they are free to make their own decisions. Such an experience depends in its turn on what local and national governments do or fail to do as far as providing or preserving a suitable environment is concerned.

Now, the process of differentiation of the demands based on diverse political orientations and the effective exclusion from formal politics of demands based on one of these major orientations has involved changes in the nature of formal politics in Britain – some of which will be discussed below. For the moment it is sufficient to point out that the above alliance has enabled the Labour Party to adapt itself to the increasing centralization of the British economy and in particular has enabled the party to adapt to, rather than to resist, the centralization. These changes in the economy, and the adaptation of political organizations to them, affect both the political environment of those in the middle-class areas and the ability of local and national government to preserve it. In this respect it will be argued that the political experience of these people is increasingly less compatible with the above orientation. Thus this orientation has been instrumental in creating the conditions of its own destruction.

The local processes of change discussed above, therefore, can affect the way politics is experienced in two ways: directly, through the effective political isolation of many of the working class and hence through the sorts of political demands which are expressed within the formal machinery of politics; indirectly, through changes in the economy and in the activities of local and national government which these processes have helped to make possible. It is impossible of course completely to separate these two types of effect, and although they will be discussed separately, a certain amount of overlap must be expected. The implications of these developments for the future shape of British politics, in the most general sense of the term, will be considered here and in the final chapter.

Consensus Politics

It is clear that the changes in the pattern of active membership of the Labour Party cannot be treated as if they represent simply a change in personnel. On the contrary, this change in personnel is both cause and consequence of the increasing domination of the political orientation attributed to the middle-class areas. Here it was argued that a vicious circle of cause and effect was in operation: change in active membership increasing the strength of a particular orientation within the party and thereby making the local party more attractive to members from the middle-class areas and less attractive to those elsewhere, leading to a further change in personnel, and so on.

As a result of these changes, not only has a particular orientation towards politics come to dominate discussion within the Labour Party, but the determination of local policy is now very largely in the hands of activists in the more middle-class areas. Thus, at the local level, the interests of the middle-class areas dominate the Labour Party in two very different senses: at the level of the general forms of political discussion by treating the details, the particular cases, as technical or administrative rather than political matters; at the level of the particular policy adopted.

Activists, ex-activists, or those who might have been activists may, therefore, feel estranged from the Labour Party in two respects. On the one hand the dominant forms of political discussion, the ways in which demands must be articulated if they are to be recognized as political, are not particularly suited to their concerns. On the other hand, over and above this particular limitation which distorts but does not entirely prevent their expression, these concerns must compete with those of the larger and stronger parties of the more prosperous areas.

Furthermore the dominant political orientation, which dominates the other major parties also, generates, or at least allows, a style of political debate in which disputes can be presented as if they were technical rather than strictly political. Thus opponents of a particular proposal are free to attack it at the level of principle or at the level of the means appropriate to the agreed and desired end.

Two consequences are particularly worth noting. On the one hand political debate is able to centre more round questions of means and less round those of ends, and political parties can compete at the level of competence while effectively keeping many issues out of politics. In practice, of course, differences in administrative machinery can mean that the same apparent policy could have very different consequences. This, in effect, is the second point, for the complexity of the administrative aspects (which are primarily a matter for specialists) allow for local or national government action to be judged in terms of its promise rather than its practical consequences* – at least by those who are not at the receiving end of these actions and often by many of those who are.

In this situation it is easy for the various parties to play the game of stealing each others' clothes. Thus a policy which appears to be winning support for one party will often be adopted in general terms by other parties also. This does not commit the various parties to the same action if elected, rather it commits them to similar vague generalities.

The appearance of near-consensus in local and, for that matter, national politics is hardly surprising. It operates both at the level of general political orientation, of conceptions of the sort of thing politics is, and at the level of particular politics. Since all major parties are dominated locally by the middle-class areas and since it is the activists from these areas, and the local leaders, who provide the national party leadership with their impression of the 'feeling in the party', such policy differences as exist will be more easily distinguished by people in these areas. For these people the differences stand out against the taken-for-

* Thus, for example, attempts at government regulation of industry may be supported by those who approve such government control in principle even though the practical effect is to strengthen the position of the apparently regulated group. For a discussion of such ineffective regulation see A. A. Rogow & P. Shore, *The Labour Government and British Industry*, London, 1955.

granted background of an agreed general orientation. People in the more working-class areas on the other hand often see very little difference between these policies. Thus, for those who accept the dominant orientation, it is only the areas of dispute between the parties that are problematic. For the rest the areas of agreement are also problematic and differences within these areas therefore appear less significant.

The apparent growth of consensus is, then, directly related to the political isolation of a fairly substantial section of the population. Here again there is a vicious circle of cause and effect. This form of political consensus, or near-consensus, allows for two very different types of political apathy. On the one hand is the apathy of those who are reasonably content with things as they are, who don't really care too much which party gets elected – because they will be all right either way. On the other hand is the apathy of those who are poorly served by the present political system, who have little reason to accept this consensus. Here again it doesn't matter too much which party gets elected because neither of them can be expected to do very much about the things that matter.

This latter is the apathy of the politically isolated, of many of those in the more working-class areas of Britain's towns and cities. Here there is at best a grudging acceptance of the present system, not because the system is particularly good, but rather because there appears to be no real alternative.

This consensus operates not only at the level of policy, where in fact a certain amount of debate is still possible, but also at the more general level of what is to count, or not to count, as political. Thus, from the point of view of those who accept the consensus, the demands and concerns expressed by the politically isolated appear at best to be non-political. At worst they appear as stupid, irrational or irresponsible.*

* cf. Chapter Four.

The consensus then is not an open and all-inclusive one. It is closed and exclusive. This has consequences for the way in which politics is perceived both by those who remain within and for those who are without the present consensus.

The Polarization of Formal Politics

The most obvious point here is that it is becoming increasingly difficult to interpret the Labour/Conservative polarization of formal politics in class terms. It was argued in Chapter One that such an interpretation is often implicit in the work of sociologists and political scientists who feel the need to account for the 'working-class conservative' while the working-class Labour voter possess no such problem.

Something of such a class polarization can, of course, still be seen at the level of electoral support and even, though to a far lesser extent, at the level of active membership. Some elements of class polarization can even be found at the level of policy (or rather of policy pronouncement) but these have declined since the war and remain now only in touches of rhetoric to be produced on suitably solemn occasions.

It is thus even more difficult now than it may once have been to see the Labour Party as the political arm of some working-class movement or, in contrast, to see militant capitalism in the activities of the Conservative Party. In many respects it seems more reasonable to claim that Britain now possesses two major, and one minor, middle-class parties.

It is important not to exaggerate either the extent or the rate of this change. Of course the Labour Party has never been a purely working-class organization and it cannot, therefore, be claimed that it has changed from being a working-class to a middle-class party. The situation here, as the earlier section of this chapter shows, is far more complex. What has happened, rather, is that certain types of interest have been squeezed out of the general coalition represented by the Labour Party.

This change is significant not simply because it has happened but also because it has become increasingly apparent that it has happened. To some extent, of course, the gradual nature of this change may have obscured it. It may, nevertheless, be recognized in the language used by party spokesmen and in the actions of the party, more particularly since the 1964 election.

This change in the way the Labour Party is perceived implies also a change in the perception of the Labour/ Conservative polarization and therefore of the nature of formal politics in Britain.

It is difficult, then, to use class consciousness as an explanation of Labour voting or of more active support – except perhaps in terms of a traditional allegiance. Some sort of traditional allegiance may indeed be particularly useful as an explanation of the relative stability to date of voting patterns. However, and this has been the main burden of the argument so far, such traditional allegiances are themselves breaking down, as are the political and economic conditions which may once have maintained them.

If, for example, one votes Labour because this is the party of the working class this necessarily involves the belief that the Labour Party will act in the interests of the working class – not perhaps in every single case, but in general. Such beliefs are subject to change, and these changes depend on the past behaviour of both the national and the local party organization and on what the interests of the working class are thought to be. Thus the decline in Labour support in the more working-class areas of our cities, without incidentally any particular increase in Con- servative support, can hardly be interpreted as showing that voters in these areas no longer see themselves as working class. It may, however, indicate that many of them no longer see any good reason for voting Labour or indeed for voting at all.

To the extent that the Labour Party no longer appears as

a class party (of the working class) it is difficult to see the
Conservatives as the party of the middle classes. Class has
been taken, or rather forced, out of politics. This is clear,
for example, in the case of the problem of housing which,
as far as the structure of formal politics is concerned, is not
a working class problem. For, although it largely affects
working-class people and may be seen by them in class
terms, there are many others in the working class who are
not affected by it and, it seems, do not behave as if this were
their problem.

However, while it is getting more and more difficult for
working-class people to vote Labour, or for middle-class
people to vote Conservative or Liberal, on the basis of some
class loyalty, it is still, of course, possible for them to find
reasons for voting one way or the other – particuarly for
those who are happy to operate within the overall consensual orientation to politics.

The apparent class nature of politics had, for very many
people, effectively eliminated the problem of voting choice:
one voted for the appropriate party often without even
needing to consider the particular policies offered. In this
respect, then, class has been a great stabilizing factor in
British politics throughout this century – or at least since
the disintegration of the once powerful Liberal Party.

While, of course, many people still vote in this fashion,
the progressive removal of class from politics and from the
way politics is perceived opens the way for an increasing
fluidity of formal political life. There is now a problem of
voting choice and this situation leads to two opposing
tendencies: the increasing importance of actual policy; and
the increasing importance of manufactured party images
now that the old class images are wearing out.

On the first point the electorate are now less likely to
vote out of a sense of class solidarity and more in terms of a
sober calculation of material advantages. At first sight then,
since the older (basically class) loyalties no longer provide
a reliable guide, it seems that people are being increasingly

forced to vote according to their assessment of the relative merits of the competing parties. This represents a change in people's psychological orientation towards politics, or at least towards the party battle. However, this change cannot be explained in terms of the characteristics of the individual voters concerned. Rather it is a response to change in the nature of the party battle.

It is ironic that such an assessment is forced on the voters at a time when, in part for the reasons discussed above, the political ends proclaimed by party leaders bear little relation to the practical consequences of their action. To a large extent, of course, this has always been the case but, in a situation where class divisions appear to be important, the disparity between promise and practice appears to be (relatively) unimportant in comparison with the fact that Labour represents one side and the Conservatives represent the other.

Since such larger and more general criteria are no longer available the disparity between promise and practice assumes a greater importance – even though politicians may in fact be no less reliable than they have ever been. Politicians cannot be trusted and this fact is more relevant than it may once have been. Hence the importance of manufacturing the right image for the party. For such an image would provide a basis for electoral support which, to a large extent, is independent of what the party actually does. This emphasis on image-making makes it even more difficult for members of the electorate to trust what politicians say. Even the images cannot be trusted.

Thus, oversimplifying somewhat, the situation is as follows: it is increasingly important for the elector that he be able to choose between the parties on the basis of the competing programmes which they offer, but it is increasingly difficult to place any reliance on these programmes and the elector is instead invited to rely on an image which is manufactured for this purpose and which he knows to be so manufactured. While, in other words, rational choice appears to be called for, the basis for such a rational choice no longer exists.

Since then, for an increasing number of people, neither the old party loyalties nor the basis for a rational political choice exist, we should expect to find an increase in that instability of political commitment which has been reflected in opinion polls since Labour last came to power.

More significant, perhaps, is the fact that this situation tends to generate an estrangement from politics even among those who accept the dominant, consensual orientation outlined above. This should not be confused with the estrangement of the politically isolated in the working-class areas. The one reflects at best a grudging and rather hostile acceptance of the status quo and a recognition that politics has nothing to offer. This will shortly be discussed more fully.

The other sort of estrangement is vastly different. Here there is a basic acceptance of the dominant definitions of politics, of the sorts of things that politics is about. It is the machinery that is wrong: the present party structure is in-effective and inefficient, the politicians often cannot be trusted to get things done or in what they say. A similar (in some respects) distrust of politicians characterized the Fourth Republic in France before de Gaulle took over. However a similar (temporary) solution is unlikely in Britain, for the situation in other respects is very different. The question of what comes next will be considered more fully in the final chapter.

The Effects of Political Isolation

The situation of the politically isolated, of those who are excluded from the overall consensus, is rather different. Here it is not only the Labour Party which is perceived as not representing their interests. Rather it is the whole apparatus of formal politics from which they are excluded and which they perceive as excluding them, or as having nothing, or very little, to offer.

However, even though formal politics has little to offer, this little may be better than nothing at all. Thus it is still possible for people in this position to be active in formal politics or to vote in local or national elections. The activists may well have some residual attachment to the Labour Party and are likely to have a basically manipulative attitude towards local councillors and party leaders and, for that matter, towards those who are active in the small political sects or factions. Such individuals, sects and factions are there to be used, to be dropped when there is no further use for them.*

For the vast majority, however, the rewards of such activity are hardly worth the effort involved. Many, of course, still vote but it notable that in both national and local elections the turnout is much lower in the more working-class areas of cities than it is elsewhere, and that this turnout has steadily declined since some time in the late 1940s or early 1950s. Here the vicious circle is one of decline rather than growth. The political apathy and estrangement from formal politics tends to be self-sustaining.

Thus a few remain committed to some sort of action within the formal political system. Others, a very small minority, move out of formal politics into the already existing political sects and factions. The vast majority, however, become apathetic, in the strongest of the two senses outlined above and move, to a greater or lesser extent, out of formal politics altogether. This may well involve acceptance of the evaluation of their concerns as non-political by those who remain within the consensus. Some may even accept the implied stigma and view their own political concerns (and perhaps even themselves) as irrational.

An increasing number are becoming involved as 'clients' with the Ministry of Social Security and various social work agencies. Such agencies tend to emphasize their role

* cf. Chapter Five.

in 'helping people to help themselves'. Those who remain in contact with the agency or agencies are thus led to see themselves not only as needing help (which can be explained in terms of illness or bad luck) but as being unable to make use of such help when it arrives – i.e. as personally inadequate. In addition, then, to the feeling of irrationality which derives from their experience of politics, a growing minority are led to see themselves as useless and helpless as well. The growing integration of these agencies and their developing contacts with, say, the local housing department, are likely to intensify these developments.[2]

Many more, however, see themselves not as irrational but rather as having concerns and interests which are simply nothing to do with politics – for the world of party politics provides, for most people, the only available definition of what is political. Such disaffection from, and disgust at, politics does not prevent people from doing something about their concerns. It may prevent them from defining their action as political.

The housing issue is of particular interest here. However much the Labour Party may once have functioned as an instrument for the exercise of local political power by the working class – in particular for working-class control over the housing market – the increasing political isolation of those in the poor housing areas means, among other things, that the party has become increasingly less effective in this respect.

Thus it is not surprising that the last few years have seen the growth of tenants' associations or community organizations and, more recently, squatters' groups, which are thought by many of those involved to be non-political, and which certainly operate outside the structure of party politics.

Such developments have a wider significance than might appear from the present concentration on the housing issue. It was argued above* that social democratic parties function

* In Chapters Two and Six.

as mechanisms of social control by restraining, reinterpreting or channelling, the demands of their membership and supporters. Such social control, such restraint, is effective only to the extent that the parties give sufficient satisfaction to the demands of their supporters as to prevent them from attempting other solutions to their problems.

The control by the party of its members or supporters and the control of the party by its members are therefore inter-related. The party's control over its members or supporters declining, in the long run, with the members' control over their party. Because of the particular nature of the political concerns of many members and supporters, and many more ex-members and ex-supporters, in the more working-class areas this exclusion from control over even their local party represents a more general exclusion from the party political system. Certainly there is no other party within this system to which they can turn.

As the tenants' associations, squatters and so on indicate, this does not mean the end of action which, in the broad sense of the term is political. What it does mean is that the action takes place outside of politics, as this term is normally understood. The way is open therefore for all sorts of 'political' activity of the politically isolated outside the sphere of formal politics.

Within the formal political system in which the basic units of political organization are the local government ward, the urban or rural district, and the constituency, the boundaries of these basic units cut across many other possible interest groups and therefore tend to inhibit other forms of political organization. Thus, for example, within party politics people are organized as residents in this ward or that constituency rather than as tenants or home-owners, workers or managers, professionals or employers, and so on.

To the extent that people can accept and operate within this dominant consensual form of politics these other possible forms of 'political' organization are inhibited. Conversely, to the extent that people are excluded from this consensus and recognize this exclusion, these other forms of organization become possible.

Housing is an obvious case in point, for in many areas people are organizing as corporation tenants, or simply as tenants, often in a way which cuts across the boundaries formally imposed by the political system. Since most of those who are politically isolated in this way are workers as well as tenants, and often work in industries where they are poorly paid and where the demand for labour is declining or likely to decline in the near future, there is a possibility even of local organization on an occupational or class basis. The situation here is complicated by the existence of trade unions – although in some cases they may provide the basis for other type of organization.*

In any case it seems likely that such forms of apparently extra-political activity will become more common in the future. In theory this could be avoided if the formal political organizations were made more effectively democratic. In practice, since those who accept the dominant orientation towards politics tend to see those who do not as irrational or irresponsible or, even worse, as 'politically motivated' it is difficult to see how this could possibly be brought about.

Such extra-political activity does not at present pose any great threat to the existing political and economic system. In part this is because many of those involved tend to accept current definitions of politics and therefore tend to view their own action as being non-political, as being concerned only with a particular issue. The rejection of the present political system, which is implicit in such action, is, as yet, merely implicit. There is no attempt to replace it with something else. Except for a very small minority, the only conceptual frameworks available which can relate their own concerns to the overall society are provided from within the party system. The future then depends on how

* At the time of writing (August/September 1969), for example G.L.C. tenants over a wide area of East London appear to be extending their organization with the help of the dockers' occupational network.

the parties react to this extra-political activity. In particular, attempts may be made to defuse the situation by offering some form of participation or by the appointment of community development officers. In some cases this may prove successful but in other cases, particularly with respect to housing, the tension seems likely to continue.

The longer the political isolation continues the more likely it is that the rejection of the present political system will be made explicit. This, as we shall see later, is particularly likely in the case of the children of those who are now isolated.

The Personal and the Political

Much of the argument of this book has centred on the dominance of a political orientation which, I have claimed, derives from the experience of a strict separation between personal and political matters. This type of experience has been, and to a large extent still is, prevalent among the secure middle classes and among many of those who, while in terms of occupation are not middle class, have been able to adopt, or to expect to adopt, many features of the middle-class life-style. Home ownership or the prospect of home ownership has been particularly important here, although a secure tenancy in a middle-class area or even in the higher status corporation estates may also be compatible with this type of experience.*

The political orientation based on this type of experience is one which emphasizes a distinction between broad policy matters, which are strictly political, and the administration of the broad policy. Among some sections of the middle classes, however, there has been a growing concern with participation (their own) in, for example, town planning,

* There is thus a germ of truth in the contention that some of the more prosperous members of the working class saw themselves as middle class (cf. the comments on embourgoisement in Chapter One). It is a mistake however to claim that this should lead people to vote Conservative.

the siting of new airports and even in industry. This latter is found particularly within the Liberal Party but also occurs within the Labour and, to a very slight extent, the Conservative Parties. This suggests that the underlying type of experience (that of local and national government as securing and maintaining an environment within which properly personal decisions may be made) is under pressure as a result of political and economic change. There is not the space here to consider the impact of such changes on the life styles and experiences of the middle classes in any great detail. But it is possible to make a few points.

I shall comment, then, on developments connected with three aspects of the experience of personal decision-making within a secure environment. There is, of course, much more to be said but it will not be said here. These aspects relate to employment, housing and transport. Of these only housing has been discussed in previous chapters where, among other things, it was argued that home ownership (or the prospect or possibility thereof) was significant both in itself (because it does provide a secure base for personal decision) and as symbolizing a number of other more widespread rights. Similar feelings of security and of rights may be generated in the other areas also.*

As far as employment is concerned the middle classes have been able to experience an environment, both within the employing organization and in the more general economic sphere, in which they were reasonably secure and in which change was something for them as individuals to decide upon. The position and responsibility of the individual is even more important in the experience of the self-employed professional. In many other individual cases, of course, such experience has been based on illusion. However, it has generally had a sufficiently widespread basis, in fact, for it to provide the dominant middle-class

---

* Of course the experience of this security or of these rights may be illusory. What matters, for the purposes of this discussion, is the experience, not whether it has any basis in fact.

view of the world of employment.³ Here again it is not important that people should actually change their job as a result of personal decision. What matters is that they should feel able to do this and that the economic environment is one in which their right to do this is preserved.

In this respect the experience of those of the working class or lower middle class who shared the basic middle-class orientation to politics has more obviously been based on illusion. Even where the job itself is reasonably secure the experience on the job is rarely one of individual autonomy. Thus the experience of individual autonomy and security is generally possible for these people only if the whole world of work is somehow divorced from the rest of their everyday life. Those in this position are therefore particularly vulnerable.

For many of the middle classes themselves, particularly those in larger organizations, the experiences of personal autonomy on the job and of career planning by the individual concerned are both beginning to break down. Here the growing use of modern management techniques on the managers themselves, including in many cases the deliberate planning of career structures, and the growing impact of computers are particularly significant. Furthermore the job security of managerial employees at all levels is increasingly vulnerable with the growth of mergers and takeovers on the one hand and the rationalization of management structures on the other. Of course non-managerial employees are even more vulnerable, but this vulnerability is a permanent feature of working-class life. Managers, on the other hand, have been able to expect a considerable degree of job security, with dismissal only in cases of gross incompetence and often not even then. The realization that they can now lose their job through no fault of their own, something the working class have always lived with, can be frightening.

This may not matter too much to those who are successful (while they are successful) or to those in currently expanding specialisms (e.g. computer programming). For many of the rest, however, areas of decision which are, so they feel, properly left to the individual concerned are being invaded. Furthermore this invasion often now comes not from within the organization concerned but from a government agency (the Prices and Incomes Board).

In many cases this breakdown of middle-class orientation is reflected in aggressive, and sometimes militant, trade unionism. In many other cases, however, this is not possible. Here there is simply insecurity where security should be.

While home ownership represents both a type of security and the right of an individual to decide on the area in which he, and his family, should live, together with all that goes with this right, car ownership represents both a type of freedom and the right of an individual to decide on when and where he may travel. Both sets of rights are often, of course, severely limited but these limitations have generally been of such a type that the individuals concerned have not experienced the constraints as being exercised by any particular body. Thus, for example, their freedom of movement may be limited by traffic conditions. While they may blame the government for not spending more on roads they do not experience this limitation as being directly imposed by government.

Both sets of rights are vulnerable to attack by planning and often the attacks themselves are related. The right to travel when and where one feels like it has been exercised by an increasing number of people year by year. This of course, affects the public transport services in two respects by adversely affecting the traffic conditions in which they operate; by the fact that the views of members of the corporation transport committee tend to be conditioned by their own use of private transport. Hence public transport services in general have deteriorated (at least from the point of view of the user) and more and more of those who could afford it have moved on to private transport.

This process severely limits the rights (to travel, to freedom from noise, dirt, fumes etc.) of those, particularly in the central working-class areas, who have to rely on public transport. Furthermore, there are now so many exercising their rights to travel that they severely limit each other, and that local government is being forced to impose direct restrictions on this right – and there are even suggestions of prohibitive road pricing in some areas.

At the same time there is a growth of car parks, one-way street systems and urban motorways. While, of course, the inner working-class areas are the most obvious victims of these developments their effects are being increasingly felt even in the outer middle-class areas.

These latter effects are in any case compounded by the continuing growth of government and industrial planning. The planning machinery set up, in the first instance, to cope with the devastation (of war, old age, neglect) in the inner areas of cities and towns, and to provide outer suburbs for at least some of the working class, is now moving outwards and linking up with other planning bodies to form a stronger and more effective regional and national planning network.

The growth of all this planning machinery is increasingly having its effect on the middle-class areas – although a majority are still immune and a minority are able to buy immunity. In its earlier stages, much of this machinery was set up under the influence of the dominant middle-class orientations. Thus there were matters of general principle, of broad policy outlines which could reasonably be discussed by laymen, and questions of detail which were basically matters of administration, to be dealt with by specialists. Furthermore, in its formative and most vulnerable period this form of organization was defended by those in the middle-class areas against attack by many in the working-class areas who were not content to leave details, which directly affected them, to specialists.

It is this form of organization which is now, and will be

increasingly, at work on the middle-class areas. While those in the working-class areas who have been subject to this machinery have long experienced their rights as rather fragile, and local government as external, constraining and coercive, people in the middle-class areas are more attached to their rights (which are in any case experienced as much stronger than the corresponding working-class ones) and have been used to the experience of government as providing basic environmental services and leaving them alone.

Thus the middle class experience of security and basic unquestioned rights is now less reliable, more fragile than it once was. Of course the number whose position is under attack from all directions is still very, very small. However there is a growing minority whose position is under attack from one direction or another and a much larger group who are aware of such attacks without directly experiencing them.

In particular, then, for more and more people in the middle-class areas, the basic political orientations which I have attributed to them are likely to change in the face of their growing insecurity. There are two fairly obvious responses. On the one hand, since politicians are increasingly objects of distrust, it may be thought that what is wrong is the calibre of the men in public life, that men of a higher calibre would be able to stand up to their advisers and bureaucrats and to keep the planners under control. Measures must be taken to attract high quality people to public life; by paying local councillors (or at least some of them) and by paying M.P.s more. On the other hand there may be a demand for more participation.

It is difficult to believe that either of these will be found to be particularly satisfactory. It has been argued above that the distrust of politicians is not to any great extent a consequence of their personal qualities. Rather it is a consequence of the decline of the class basis of party loyalty and of the increasing use of manufactured party images.

Measures taken to attract high quality people can hardly improve matters in this latter respect. On the contrary they allow for the increasing reliance on the 'high calibre' image. This image requires that party leaders devote themselves as much, or even more, to the cultivation of the appearance of expertise, of taking energetic steps, as to doing what their apparent expertise fits them to do.

With respect to participation the situation is rather different although, as in the former case, it is at least as popular amongst politicians as it is with the public at large.*

In many cases, of course, participation in planning may satisfy many of the individuals concerned. In other cases, however, the interests of private individuals in the area affected may come into direct and obvious conflict with those of the increasingly powerful state and industrial organizations.

In such cases the political strength of those in the middle-class areas is now limited by two important factors. On the one hand, by helping to defeat the political demands of the working-class areas they have directly contributed to the strength of the party bureaucracy and indirectly to that of the state. Since, on the other hand, the working-class areas have been effectively removed from politics, activists in

---

* The proposals, of course, seem particularly designed to appeal to the middle classes. The report of the Skeffington Committee, for example, nowhere considers the peculiar position of those who are tenants of the local planning authority. *People and Planning* (Report of the Committee on Public Participation in Planning), H.M.S.O., London, 1969. The National Executive of the Labour Party are so concerned with this issue that they have launched a new scheme for giving the party's rank-and-file more say in policy making. Introducing the scheme, 'Participation '69', the General Secretary pointed out that: 'One of our proudest claims has always been that we are a democratic movement, hammering out our policies by argument and debate until a majority view emerges.' He went on to add that: 'what has been needed is the opportunity to involve local groups in the working out of our policies.' The party in other words has been democratic without involving the rank-and-file in decision making. *The Times*, 2 October 1967.

the middle-class areas are no longer so important as allies of the party leaderships and have, in any case, been instrumental in their growing autonomy. Thus in the event of conflict with industrial or state bureaucracies their political position is weaker now than it has been.

It is tempting here to apply Lefebvre's comments on the France of 1968:

The state ... desires (perhaps sincerely) participation so as to fill the void which it has created; [but] the state cannot bring about effective participation since it makes all decisions itself. ... It is quite understandable that in this paradoxical situation the authorities are feverishly engaged in filling the void they have created; this has been their only creative activity. They have eliminated all participation: Long live participation! They have monopolised decision making: Long live the people who make decisions! They have discredited Parliament: Long live parliamentary democracy!*

Of course the situation in Britain is different: Parliament appears to be more effective and the party battle with its competing leaderships allows for a greater vicarious participation than was possible in de Gaulle's France. The void in Britain is perhaps less extensive and is certainly less visible as yet. It nevertheless exists and seems likely to grow.

* H. Lefebvre, *The Explosion: Marxism and the French Upheaval*, London, 1967, pp. 47, 52.

8 Conclusions

This book has been concerned with changes in working-class involvement in formal political life since the war. In particular it has been argued that these changes have been of two distinct, but nevertheless closely related, types. On the one hand there has been, in many areas, an absolute decline in voting and in other forms of orthodox political activity. On the other hand the close association between party and social class has itself declined and, with the progressive disappearance of the class polarization of formal politics, there has been a decline in political activity resulting from identification with, and commitment to, the interests of the working class as such.

The argument has remained primarily at the level of grass-roots politics, beginning with the relationships between the political structure and the ecology of the city. Of particular significance here was the relationship between housing conditions, and related features, and the political influence and interests of different areas. Differences of interest operate both within and between parties at the city level and the differences between the more middle-class and the more working-class sections of the city were emphasized throughout.

Political interests and political concerns are not, and cannot be treated as, innate characteristics of the people concerned. I have attempted to relate differences in political interests and in overall political orientations to differences in the life-experiences of the relevant social groups. This, of course, involves a certain amount of oversimplification. On the one hand, the life-experience of each individual is unique, while I have been concerned only with broad features of this experience. On the other hand political orientations relate both to people's own individual experience of government and politics, and to the dominant orientations of the social milieu in which they live. Thus working-class tenants living in middle-class areas have often been able to adopt the orientations dominant in the area. This adoption has itself been aided by the way basic units of formal political organization (ward, constituency, etc.) bring people together on the basis of area and not, say, on the basis of class position or housing situation.

Changes in the Labour Party and in the urban environment have led to the differentiation of the political demands, concerns and orientations of party members and supporters in the different areas. In this differentiation the orientations of the middle-class areas have been compatible both with the interests of the party leadership and with the response of the party organization to its own changing institutional environment. Thus local parties in the more working-class areas have come into conflict both with other local parties and with the party bureaucracy. The result of this alliance between the parties in the middle-class areas and the party bureaucracy has been a gradual shift of power within the local party, and of membership, towards these areas. The shifts of power and of membership are related in a vicious circle of decline in some areas and of growth in others.

These changes have resulted in a substantial degree of consensus between the city parties, although there may still be some important differences, and also in the political isolation of substantial sections of the population. They have also been related to developments within the national organization of the Labour Party and therefore to the nature of the Labour/Conservative polarization of British politics.

Changes at the local level in politics are intimately related to changes at other levels of the political system, and also to the increasing centralization of the British economy. While it has not been possible to discuss the effect of these latter developments on the higher levels of political organization in any detail, it is clear that they have an impact on the life-experiences of many of the electorate and can therefore affect their political orientations. On the former point it has become increasingly less meaningful to discuss the day-to-day structure of formal politics in class terms. The consequent changes in the way in which politics is perceived by many of the electorate were discussed in the last chapter.

However, while it has been necessary to consider these wider developments, the analysis has been primarily concerned with processes of change at the grass-roots level of politics. The relationship between the various levels of politics, or between different processes at a similar level, is by no means a simple one of cause and effect.

Thus, for example, government or local government policy with respect to housing may affect the grass-roots level of politics in a number of different ways. In particular it may affect the image of the party in power and, depending on its response, of the opposition. However it also has concrete effects, not necessarily those intended, on the supply of housing and the general housing situation of different sections of the population. Thereafter, through the complex chain of developments discussed earlier, these changes relate to the pattern of political activity and therefore to the sort of grass-roots pressure the party leaders have to cope with.

Developments at the higher levels of politics, then, affect the grass-roots by changing the conditions within which people act, by introducing new elements into the political situation of individuals, communities, and classes. In each case the effect depends in part on the already existing political orientations and expectations of the people concerned, and these in turn are affected by other, apparently non-political, developments. Thus, for example, the rationalization of management structures in industry limits, in many cases, that feeling of personal security which underlies the basic political orientations of the middle classes.

Furthermore the introduction of new elements into the political situation of individuals – the enormous growth, for example, of council housing in the post war years – both allows for, and leads to, the development of new political demands. These in turn affect the conditions of action of political leaders.

The relationships, then, between different levels of the political system, between the actions of different groups of people, is stable only so long as other things remain equal. Other things are rarely so obliging. In particular, as far as politics is concerned, the actions of political leaders themselves would be sufficient to ensure that other things cannot remain equal for very long. Obvious examples, which have been discussed at several points, are the changes in the housing or employment situations which have been brought about by political action, and the growing centralization of the British economy which has, at the very least, been aided and encouraged by successive governments.

Other government policies, other social and economic developments, have hardly been mentioned however. Yet it is clear that any complete account of political change would have to bring in many of these developments which have not been discussed here. Changes in the overall situation of the individuals concerned affect both the consequences of their action and the meaning they attach to this action.

This is not to say, of course, that the overt political actions must change or that such changes will always be recognized. Thus, returning to the discussion of Chapter One, a Labour vote is a Labour vote whenever and wherever it is cast. This apparent stability is not entirely illusory but it nevertheless masks many changes both in the meaning the vote has for the voter and in the organization he supports. In this situation someone, say, who votes Labour time after time may well appear to be a loyal supporter of the Party and may even think of himself as such. The loyalty, however, is not towards the party, it is towards the party label. The basis even of this loyalty is continually shifting – or else becoming increasingly remote from the real world in which the vote is cast. In such a development the final steps, say, from Labour voting to non-Labour voting, or non-voting, may appear as a response to quite trivial events. The study of political behaviour in terms of overt and easily labelled actions (voting Labour, Liberal, Conservative) rather than the meanings of these actions for the voter, serves to strengthen this illusion.

No attempt has been made here to deal with the full range of political developments or with all of the relationships between the political, economic and social spheres. Rather I have attempted to identify and to clarify some of the processes involved in the changing nature of British politics since the last war. Other processes are of course involved. Some were discussed briefly in the last chapter which attempted to locate the local developments within a wider context. Many others were not.

The present analysis, then, is both partial and incomplete and it cannot pretend to be otherwise. The processes discussed, however, are real enough, as are their wider implications, and must form part of any attempt to account for the nature of contemporary politics.

Before concluding with a discussion of the implications of the present analysis for the future of British politics it is necessary to comment briefly on one further point.

On the whole the present discussion has remained squarely within the context of the British situation. Yet several features of contemporary British politics, which have been discussed as if they arose out of specifically British developments, may be found elsewhere.[1]

Thus, it seems apathy, resignation and indifference characterize the political position of the working class throughout the developed industrial countries of the west today.[2] Similarly, as the quotation from Lefebvre suggests, the growing autonomy of political leaders, and of state machinery in general, which I have argued may be found in Britain, can be seen in an even more extreme form in France and, to a greater or lesser extent, throughout the industrial world.

Since these features are so widespread it might be argued that they should be explained in terms of more general characteristics of contemporary capitalist society, rather than as the outcome of the specific processes discussed in this book. It may, for example, be claimed that the apathy and political indifference of the working class is characteristic of advanced (or mature or post-) capitalist society and results from say, affluence, the ready availability of material goods, ever increasing living standards and thus of a general satisfaction with the way things are going. More pessimistically, they may be attributed to the effects of advertising, the creation and manipulation of false needs by vested interests, by, perhaps, manipulation of the language, and thus by effectively disguising real exploitation and effectively limiting the scope of human experience.[3] With explanations of this type it hardly seems necessary to specify the actual processes, the real human actions, by means of which these general features have their effect.

I would not deny the existence or the importance of some of these general characteristics. Nevertheless it is necessary to reject the suggestion that there is any opposition between explanation by general characteristics and explanation by detailed processes. Such an opposition implies that these general characteristics exist apart from, or underlie, or even cause, the type of process discussed here.

However, in spite perhaps of appearances to the contrary, these general characteristics, underlying forces and so on, exist in, and have their effect through, the real beliefs, assumptions, actions or relationships between real people. There is nowhere else.

For any particular individual, of course, the feeling that there are external and constraining social forces, that there are objective constraints within which he must act and which are independent of anything he may do, has some basis in fact. Thus, for each and every individual, the objective constraints are provided by the actions and relationships of other individuals. At the same time each individual, acting within what he believes to be his objective constraints, thereby provides one small part of the constraints on others.

The appearance of such stable and relatively immutable objective features may therefore be illusory in two respects: it is only individuals and relatively small groups of individuals who are powerless before these objective constraints; these features themselves change anyway (without, perhaps, anyone intending to change them) as a result of the sorts of processes discussed in earlier chapters.

Two points are important here. On the one hand such collective illusions make a large contribution to the relative stability of the political system; and conversely such relative stability tends to justify these collective illusions. On the other hand it is clear that explanations of this relative stability in terms of the types of general features indicated above can be trusted only if it is possible to specify the concrete processes, the types of action and social relationship, by which they have their effect. *Otherwise such proposed explanations are no more than suggestions or hypotheses – which may nevertheless tend to be self-confirming to the extent that people believe them to be correct and act accordingly.

Thus the analysis of working-class political apathy and of the growing autonomy of the state (at least as far as the population at large is concerned) presented here does not provide an alternative to explanation in terms of general propositions relating particular features of western capitalist

* I do not claim that each author should do this for himself. All that matters is that some such specification be provided.

society. On the contrary it provides an exemplification of, and a check upon, such general propositions.

In the present case the general proposition is a modified form of Michels' Iron Law – 'who says organization says oligarchy'.* The organization has been the British Labour Party and I have been particularly concerned with the position of the grass-roots members, supporters and possible supporters – or, as Michels' would have it, the masses. The present analysis, in other words, has seen the Iron Law, or rather some of its facets, in operation and has followed through its consequences at the grass-roots level and some of their wider implications.

The Iron Law of Oligarchy as formulated and elaborated by Michels represents, it would seem, merely the first act of a longer, more complex, drama – the act in which the scene is set and the main characters introduced. The play itself is a tragic farce for which an appropriate title would be 'The Decline and Fall of Social Democracy'. This does not, of course, mean the end of Social Democratic Parties any more than the collapse of feudal society meant the end of the nobility. The nobility, where it survived, did so by undergoing a complete transformation. Social Democratic Parties may do likewise.

To pursue the analogy a little further, the present discussion may be seen as an extended review concentrating mainly on the last act of the English version of this larger work. In other versions the details differ as the play is modified in accordance with different local conditions, different national cultures. The characters, the sub-plots, the nuances of timing – all these are changed to a greater or lesser extent, and they certainly appear to be different. Only the basic theme is unaltered.†

* Discussed at length in Chapter Two.
† It might be added that, in the hands of a different reviewer, the present emphasis on the crowd scenes might be replaced by a concern with a few central figures – party and industrial leaders for example. The crowd would then appear simply as a background.

Of course such analogies have their uses and their draw-backs. In the present case, for example, the play is produced, written and directed by the actors themselves – whatever they or some of their leaders may feel about the matter. Indeed these feelings are themselves part of the script. It is a mistake then to look for a nice tidy ending with the actors joining hands for the final curtain call and all going off to a party afterwards. Rather we should expect a period of transition – with some sticking to their old roles, with others moving on to new ones, and with the rest casting around, unsure of what to do next.

The processes discussed here do, however, provide some clues as to the possible shape of future developments. The decline of social democracy has involved the effective political isolation of some sections of the working class, the decline of the class polarization of politics – and therefore a change in the whole nature of formal politics which may not even be noticed by many of those who discuss politics purely in terms of the party labels. Related developments include the growth of planning (by local and national government, industrial and commercial organizations) and a large number of other social and economic changes.

In the light of these it is possible to identify a number of different situations with respect to formal political life. The earlier distinction, between general orientations to, and definitions of, politics on the one hand and specific political interests and concerns on the other, leads to a distinction between two types of estrangement from contemporary politics. One type involves a rejection, which may be more or less well-articulated, of dominant political orientations and definitions. The other involves a general acceptance of these dominant definitions together with a belief that the actual machinery is not working too well. Both situations have been discussed in the previous chapter and it is only necessary to add a few comments here.

The numbers involved in both seem likely to grow, at least in the near future, for the processes concerned are largely self-sustaining.* In particular, in addition to the polarization within formal politics, we should expect a growing polarization between formal politics on the one hand and apparently non-political action on the other.

Here it is not so much the issues raised by tenants' associations, squatters' groups and so on that are important, but the fact that the issues themselves are increasingly raised outside the formal political organizations. It is this that marks the breakdown of that social control which the Labour Party has been able to exercise over such a large section of the population – for, as I have already noted, such control is effective only to the extent that party members are so constrained by their support of, and reliance upon, the party that they attempt no other solution to their problems.

The present extent of this breakdown should not of course be exaggerated. On the one hand, in many areas, local Labour Parties themselves have organized action (such as, for example, rent strikes, resistance to bailiffs and even, in exceptional cases, industrial action) outside of the normal political channels. In such cases, however, the very fact that a ward party, and sometimes a councillor or two, was involved gave such action an exceptional character and seriously limited the range of action considered. Furthermore, other local politicians have been able to use the interests of the party as an argument against such action, or as a reason for discontinuing it.

On the other hand most of those involved in this apparently extra-political activity are themselves disaffected party activists or supporters. To a large extent, then, they rely upon the forms of action, and the constraints thereon, which they learnt as Labour activists.

Their children, particularly the teenagers of the 1960s, are in a situation which, in two important respects, is very different from that of their parents. Having missed the

* See, for example, the discussion of the effects of political isolation and of the polarization of formal politics in Chapter Seven.

political experience of their parents, the long identification with and support for Labour, they are less likely to be inhibited by a residual identification with the party or by a respect for the proper channels, for the appropriate forms of action.

Furthermore the vast majority of them have had current affairs or civics lessons in school dealing with the British Constitution, the organization of national and local government, with democracy in action. This is intended, apparently, to produce good citizens. For the children of the politically isolated, much of what they are taught in such lessons is directly contradicted by the political experience of their parents. In these cases the party game, the whole system of formal politics, appears as a confidence trick – the more so since such an effort is made by the schools to get them to believe in it. For a minority – those who pass the 11 plus, survive the streamed comprehensive, or otherwise do well – the confidence trick may appear relatively harmless – if, that is, they feel that they at least will be all right. The majority, however, learn about the confidence trick at the same time as they learn to be 'realistic' about their ambitions. For these the trick is by no means harmless: they are its intended victims just as, it may often seem, their parents were before them.

Their rejection of politics, then, is likely to be more complete and systematic than that of their parents. Here again it is important to note that the world of formal politics does at least provide a conceptual framework which places particular concerns in the context of the overall society. In the absence of a generally accepted alternative framework this rejection of politics leads to a situation where, apart from a small minority, action is concerned only with some particular issue. Or else it appears to be unmotivated – except perhaps by a rejection of the social constraints normally accepted by their elders.

For the moment, then, the situation of this section of the population is characterized by rejection, to a greater or

lesser extent, of formal politics, by relatively spasmodic
and uncoordinated apolitical action on particular issues and,
among the younger members, a whole range of apparently
irrational unmotivated and, to their elders, immoral or
amoral activities. In many cases this latter effectively
divides parents from their children and their children from
each other. Coordinated action is as yet unlikely.

The other type of political estrangement – distrust of
politicians rather than a rejection of politics – seems likely
to grow also. Here a concern with participation will often
be combined with a desire for strong, high calibre political
leadership. Participation is desirable not only because of
their own experiences (real or anticipated) with government
planning but also as a way of containing the illegitimate
and threatening activities of tenants groups and unofficial
strikers. Similarly the concern over strong, high calibre
political leadership has a double meaning. On the one hand
it relates to a concern over planning (it would be all right
if only they had the right people at the top) and a distrust
of present politicians. On the other it relates particularly
to a concern with controlling illegitimate apolitical activity,
providing leadership for youth, law and order. Often, it is
thought, strong, high calibre leadership is required in order
to control planners, to prevent government interference –
in industry, education, and so on.

The overall emphasis is likely to vary quite considerably
among this section of the population. In part, at least,
such variation seems likely to be related to the strength of
that feeling of security which underlies the sharp dichotomy
between personal and political matters. The less secure –
those in the intermediate housing situation discussed in
Chapter Four or those whose security is particularly
threatened by the processes discussed in Chapter Seven –
can be expected to emphasize the law-and-order, control,
strong leadership, aspects. However at least some of the
former group, particularly the skilled working class, may
by becoming involved in collective industrial action (or by

the possible need for such action), be led to view the apolitical activities of those in the more working-class areas more sympathetically.

The lower middle- or middle-class groups in the insecure position are likely to feel threatened from two directions. On the one hand is the illegitimate activity of many of the working class with respect to housing (why should they expect the ratepayers to subsidize them) and their irresponsible use of their organized industrial strength (thereby ruining the economy, putting the country at the mercy of foreign bankers, etc.). On the other hand is the threat from government and from large industrial and commercial organizations. There is likely to be a strong element of scapegoating in the political outlook of such groups – with blame being cast on the unofficial strikers, trade unions, bureaucracy, socialism, immigration. Here there will be support for the Great Britain Ltd approach to government which is often thought to somehow combine efficient administration with relative freedom from government interference: if the country is administered efficiently, it seems to be thought, the economy will do well and there will be no need for government interference. This view fits particularly well with the scapegoating of the unofficial striker.*

Among the more secure sections of the middle classes, of course, the situation is still very different. In particular despite a generally agreed definition of politics, there is still disagreement as to the precise issues which should come into politics and as to the types of control appropriate in law and order issues. It is here, if anywhere, that the belief

* It is of course a mistake to blame government interference either on poor trade figures (and therefore the unions) or on the Labour Government. Such interference is rather a concommittant of the process of planning by large scale industry (private or public). In this respect the Great Britain Ltd approach can only serve to increase the extent of government interference in everyday life. See, for example, the discussions of planning in J. K. Galbraith, *The New Industrial State*, London, 1967, or P. Baran & P. Sweezy, *Monopoly Capital*, London, 1968.

in orthodox politics (both in general definitions and in present organizational forms) survives. The politics of this section of the population would require much fuller treatment than can possibly be given to it here. However it should be noted that the growth of national and local government planning and continuing economic centralization are likely to make increasing inroads on this section in the future.

Once again the children, or at least a minority of them, are in a different position. One aspect only of this situation need be mentioned here. A minority of these children, sharing perhaps something of their parents' distrust of politicians and something of the feeling that it is a confidence trick, receive a high level of education which, for some of them, no longer leads to the secure future it would once have done (or which it is thought to have done), and which exposes them to definitions of, and orientations towards, politics other than those which are dominant in this society.

Thus, while the discontent of many in their age group appears as non-political (in terms of the presently dominant definitions) this minority are able to give their discontent an explicitly political form. Here again there is a certain polarization. On the one hand are those who while accepting the overall structure of society reject its specific political forms. The most striking example of this would be the Shelter organization which is explicitly political and engages in slightly unorthodox, but by no means illegitimate, activities. There are of course many other smaller, less successful, organizations based on a similar political orientation. Participation is very popular here.

On the other hand are the smaller number who reject the dominant definition of politics. This group experience their rejection of formal politics not as a rejection of politics as such but rather as a political rejection of the present system. This provides them with a conceptual framework which, whatever its weaknesses, places their specific concerns squarely in the context of the wider society. It also places a barrier between them and those whose rejection of formal politics is experienced as a rejection of politics as such.

There are, of course, all sorts of more or less vague intermediate positions between the polar types of rejection of formal politics. More significantly, the very existence of a small revolutionary group, and the publicity given to them in the press, provides an alternative definition to which those who would otherwise reject politics altogether are increasingly being exposed. The more they are condemned by orthodox politicians the more attractive they become. As against this, the fact that the revolutionary group are, relatively speaking, highly privileged is one inhibiting factor.

The above sketchy and all too brief discussion may appear to have left the future even more obscure than it was, say, at the beginning of this chapter. There are indeed many different and contradictory developments. There is on the one hand a growing rejection of the dominant definitions of, and orientations towards, politics and on the other a growing discontent with the specific organizational forms of politics (expressed in terms of participation, strong leadership, distrust of politicians, and so on). Both cover a wide range of positions: the first ranging from a half-hearted anti-political stance with residual identification with Labour, through a thorough-going rejection of politics and sometimes of many of the behavioural standards of adult life, to a specifically and self-consciously political rejection of contemporary politics.

There are all sorts of barriers between these various positions and a range of possible futures open to those who hold them. Thus the student or ex-student revolutionaries do have the option of changing sides, of becoming respectable, and of doing quite well out of it. The others, however, have little to gain from changing their own position (even if they were able to), for the structure of contemporary politics is, as I have argued at length, such as to exclude effective consideration of their concerns or interests. This difference in possible futures is the basis of one of the barriers between the groups.*

As against these developments there is a growing concern with the present organizational forms of politics – with the party system of local and national government as it operates at the moment. This takes various forms: relatively humane (talk of participation, treating delinquency as illness); technocratic (talk of efficiency, productivity, technological revolution, need for experts); more or less authoritarian (talk of strong leadership, Great Britain Ltd, discipline against unofficial strikers, teenagers, students); or various combinations of these.

Finally there are the large numbers who are relatively apathetic, who are more or less content with their present situation – often only in comparison with those who are even worse off – and the others who play the party game seriously, according to the rules. The position of these latter is, as we saw in the last chapter, under attack from several directions.

It is clear, of course, that the future does not depend simply on the present numbers involved in the various positions indicated above. Thus the relative strengths of the various forms of concern with the present party system depends, in part, on the ways in which different sections of the population experience threats to their position, and this in turn is dependent on the activities of various planning bodies, on the extent and type of industrial reorganization, and so on.

The ranks of the politically isolated are likely to gain recruits from both the lower middle-/skilled working-class areas and, to a lesser extent, even from the middle class – again depending on the activities of government and industrial organizations. Those in this position may be more

* I do not mean to suggest that these barriers cannot be overcome, but it is clearly not inevitable that they will be.

or less active in their rejection of politics depending in part on the economic situation. Furthermore it is entirely possible that, for a time, various forms of officially sponsored participation will be able to take over the social control functions once carried out by Labour Party. To the extent that it is effective in this respect, participation seems likely to further devalue (where this is still possible) the present system of party politics.

Thus while it seems likely that the numbers involved in both broad types of estrangement from contemporary politics are likely to grow, it is difficult to say much about either the rate of change or the precise shape of future developments. In the absence of violent economic changes it is tempting to predict that the present party game will continue to be played for some time to come. In common with other mass spectator sports, however, it can be expected to resort increasingly to gimmicks in order to draw the crowds. It would be a mistake, however, to ignore the fragility (which itself is likely to increase) of this apparent stability.

Nevertheless, while the future is unclear at the grassroots level, several of the other processes discussed above must be expected to continue. The centralization of the economy, the interpenetration of government and industry (and more generally of all major institutional areas), the spread of planning, the autonomy of political leaders (as against their rank-and-file) – all these are irreversible as far as action which can be taken within the present political system is concerned.

What, it may be asked, can we do to preserve democracy? Nothing. That option is no longer available, if indeed it ever was in a society which allows, as ours does, such high concentrations of power to remain in so few hands. The rhetoric and the ritual remain and there are many even now who can find a use for them.

For the rest there remains a simpler question: what can we do? Here again there is an obvious answer: we can choose sides. On the whole those whose estrangement from politics is of the less radical type seem likely to side with those who presently wield effective power. They, at least, can offer the appearance of security, even while destroying its real content, and there are many available scapegoats. Those whose estrangement is the more radical have less choice in the matter. Many are already victims and have had their side chosen for them. They alone can choose whether to recognize this.

There are other possibilities of course. We can bury our heads in the sands of political rhetoric. Or we can simply look the other way. Both courses are likely to prove popular in years to come for they offer many short term attractions. In the long run they have little to recommend them.

Notes

INTRODUCTION

1. R. Rose, 'Class and Party Divisions: Britain as a Test Case', *Sociology*, vol. 2, no. 2, 1965, pp. 131–2.
2. *The Times*, 9 October 1969.
3. Anon. Quoted, with approval, by S. Lynd in 'Historical Past and Existential Present', T. Roszak, *The Dissenting Academy*, London, 1969, p. 105.
4. Taken from M. R. Stein, 'The Eclipse of Community' in A. J. Vidich, J. Bensman, M. R. Stein, *Reflections on Community Studies*, New York, 1964, p. 215.

CHAPTER ONE

1. See, for example, Gallup Poll 'Voting Behaviour in Britain'. In R. Rose (ed), *Studies in British Politics*, London, 1966. J. Blondel, *Voters, Parties and Leaders*, London, 1963.
2. A. Campbell, et al., *The American Voter*, New York, 1960. H. Tingsten, *Political Behaviour*, London, 1937.
3. *Socialist Commentary*, February, 1969.
4. F. Bealey, et al., *Constituency Politics*, London, 1965. A. Birch, *Small Town Politics*, London, 1959.
5. See Hindess, *Attitudes of the Conservative and Labour Parties towards the Coal Industry* (unpublished diploma thesis), Liverpool, 1964.
6. P. Willmot and M. Young, *Family and Kinship in East London*, London, 1957.

CHAPTER TWO

1. See, for example, the discussion in P. Gay, *The Dilemma of Democratic Socialism*, New York, 1962.

2. See, for example, the discussion in R. T. McKenzie, *British Political Parties*, London, 1964.

CHAPTER THREE

1. See for example, E. W. Burgess and D. J. Bogue (eds.), *Contributions to Urban Sociology*, Chicago, 1964. The argument of this section owes much to the approach developed by Rex and Moore in their study of race relations. J. Rex and R. Moore, *Race, Community and Conflict*, London, 1963.
2. This scheme is a little oversimplified. For further details see my 'Local Elections and the Labour Vote', *Sociology*, vol. 1, no. 2, 1967.
3. Number of persons per room and number of households per dwelling are particularly useful as indicators of urban structure. cf. E. Gittus 'An Experiment in the Definition of Urban Sub-Area', *Transactions of the Bartlett Society*, vol. 2, 1964.
4. A. M. Rees and T. Smith, *Town Councillors: a study of Barking*, London, 1965. (Barking is a town in Essex.) L. J. Sharp, 'Elected Representatives in Local Government', *British Journal of Sociology*, vol. 13, 1962.

CHAPTER FOUR

1. For a recent example of the use of such questions see R. T. McKenzie and A. Silver, op. cit.
2. 'Our Penny Farthing Machine', supplement to *Socialist Commentary*, October, 1965.
3. cf. N. Dennis: *People and Planning*, London, 1969.
4. For a discussion of this point and of selection procedures in general see A. Ranney, *Pathways to Parliament*, London, 1965 and E. G. Janosik, *Constituency Labour Parties in Britain*, London, 1968.

CHAPTER FIVE

1. M. Toole, *Mrs. Bessie Braddock M.P.*, London, 1957, pp. 194–6. See also the account given in J. D. & E. M. Braddock, *The Braddocks*, London, 1963, pp. 90–3.
2. J. D. & E. M. Braddock, op. cit., p. 91.
3. For a discussion of spoken or written history as myth see C. Levi-Strauss, 'Overture to "Le Cru et le Cuit"', *Yale*

French Studies, no. 36/37, or E. Leach, 'The Legitimacy of Solomon', *Archives Europeans de Sociologie*, no. 7.

4. See, for example, J. D. & E. M. Braddock, op. cit., pp. 90–93.
5. 'Our Penny Farthing Machine', supplement to *Socialist Commentary*, October 1965, p. vi. This supplement gives a particularly clear statement of this type of myth.
6. See, in particular, chapter 12 of Rex and Moore, op. cit., pp. 272–285.
7. *Report of Sub-Committee on Party Organization* (Wilson Report). Published in the Annual Conference Report, 1955. Many recommendations are repeated in 'Our Penny Farthing Machine', op. cit.
8. Attitudes of campaign supporters are examined in F. Parkin, *Middle Class Radicalism*, Manchester, 1968.
9. Several such disputes are examined in A. Ranney, *Pathways to Parliament*, London, 1965, pp. 129–220, and R. J. Jackson, *Rebels and Whips*, London, 1968, pp. 201–291. Neither author is concerned with the effects of such disputes on the local parties concerned.
10. A. Ranney, op. cit., p. 159.

CHAPTER SIX

1. For a fragmentary and often inaccurate discussion of the various groups see G. Thayer, *The British Political Fringe*, London, 1965.

 Any adequate discussion would have to cover the history of the relations between the Labour Party and the Young Socialists. I have not even attempted to do this here. Relations between the Labour Party and various socialist or radical groups are discussed briefly in R. Williams (ed.), *May Day Manifesto 1968*, London 1968, pp. 155–179.
2. cf. Anderson's view that 'unionism is the prime key to the consciousness of the British Working Class' because 'the union introduces the worker into a new ideological and relational universe, however minimally. It creates its own loyalty and its own logic – a logic that leads to Labour allegiance.' See 'Problems of Socialist Strategy' in P. Anderson and R. Blackburn (eds), *Towards Socialism*, London, 1965, pp. 262–263.

3. See the discussion of the Harlow Labour Party in P. Foot, 'In the Grass-Roots of Politics', *Sunday Times*, 20 September 1968.

CHAPTER SEVEN

1. cf. P. Thoenes, *The Elite in the Welfare State*, London, 1966, pp. 125–168.
2. The significance of the processing of people at the hands of such agencies requires much fuller treatment. See in particular A. W. Gouldner, 'The Unemployed Self' in R. Fraser (ed), *Work*, vol. 2, London, 1969.
3. Compare the accounts of middle-class and working-class occupations in R. Fraser (ed), *Work*, vol. 1, London, 1968, and vol. 2, London, 1969.

CHAPTER EIGHT

1. This is already implicit in the brief reference to Popitz' study of the workers' image of society (Chapter One), and to Lefebvre's analysis of the French society of 1968 (Chapter Seven).
2. For a survey of West European findings on this point see S. Herkommer, 'Working Class Political Consciousness', *International Socialist Journal*, vol. 2, no. 7, 1965.
3. For such pessimistic explanations see H. Marcuse, *One Dimensional Man*, London, 1964.

Index